The Readers' Advisory Guide
to Genre Blends

ALA READERS' ADVISORY SERIES

The Readers' Advisory Guide to Genre Blends

Megan M. McArdle

An imprint of the American Library Association

Chicago   2015

MEGAN M. McARDLE is a librarian with more than fifteen years of experience in public libraries doing collection development and readers' advisory. She is the Science Fiction and Fantasy columnist for *Library Journal* and has a website devoted to genre blends at genrify.com.

© 2015 by the American Librar

Extensive effort has gone into ensuring the reliability of the information in this book; however, the publisher makes no warranty, express or implied, with respect to the material contained herein.

ISBNs: 978-0-8389-1256-0 (paper); 978-0-8389-1261-4 (PDF); 978-0-8389-1262-1 (ePUB); 978-0-8389-1263-8 (Kindle). For more information on digital formats, visit the ALA Store at alastore.ala.org and select eEditions.

Library of Congress Cataloging-in-Publication Data

McArdle, Megan M., 1969-
    The readers' advisory guide to genre blends / Megan M. McArdle.
        pages cm. — (ALA readers' advisory series)
    Includes bibliographical references and index.
    ISBN 978-0-8389-1256-0 (print : alk. paper) — ISBN 978-0-8389-1262-1 (epub) — ISBN 978-0-8389-1261-4 (pdf) — ISBN 978-0-8389-1263-8 (kindle)
    1. Fiction in libraries—United States. 2. Readers' advisory services—United States. 3. Reading interests—United States. 4. Fiction genres. 5. Fiction—Bibliography. I. Title.
    Z711.5.M38 2015
    026'.80883—dc23   2014020407

Cover image © Leigh Prather / Shutterstock, Inc.
Text composition by Dianne M. Rooney in the Palatino and ITC Franklin Gothic typefaces.

Printed in the United States of America

19 18 17 16 15   5 4 3 2 1

⊗ This paper meets the requirements of ANSI/NISO Z39.48-1992 (Permanence of Paper).

ALA Editions purchases fund advocacy, awareness, and accreditation programs for library professionals worldwide.

CONTENTS

APPENDIXES

SERIES INTRODUCTION

Joyce Saricks and Neal Wyatt, Series Editors

In a library world in which finding answers to readers' advisory questions is often considered among our most daunting service challenges, library staff need guides that are supportive, accessible, and immediately useful. The titles in this series are designed to be just that. They help advisors become familiar with fiction genres and nonfiction subjects, especially those they don't personally read. They provide ready-made lists of "need to know" elements such as key authors and readalikes, as well as tips on how to keep up with trends and important new authors and titles.

Written by librarians with years of RA experience who are also enthusiasts of the genre or subject, the titles in this series of practical guides emphasize an appreciation of the topic, focusing on the elements and features fans enjoy, so advisors unfamiliar with the topics can readily appreciate why they are so popular.

Because this series values the fundamental concepts of readers' advisory work and its potential to serve readers, viewers, and listeners in whatever future-space libraries inhabit, the focus of each book is on appeal and how appeal crosses genre, subject, and format, especially to include audio and video as well as graphic novels. Thus, each guide emphasizes the importance of whole collection readers' advisory and explores ways to make suggestions that include novels, nonfiction, and multimedia, as well as how to incorporate whole collection elements into displays and booklists.

Each guide includes sections designed to help librarians in their RA duties, be that daily work or occasional interactions. Topics covered in each volume include:

> The appeal of the genre or subject and information on subgenres and types so that librarians might understand the breadth and scope of the topic and how it relates to other genres and subjects. A brief history is also included to give advisors context and highlight beloved classic titles.
>
> Descriptions of key authors and titles with explanations of why they're important: why advisors should be familiar with

them and why they should be kept in our collections. Lists of readalikes accompany these core author and title lists, allowing advisors to move from identifying a key author to helping patrons find new authors to enjoy.

Information on how to conduct the RA conversation so that advisors can learn the tools and skills needed to develop deeper connections between their collections and their communities of readers, listeners, and viewers.

A crash course in the genre or subject designed to get staff up to speed. Turn to this section to get a quick overview of the genre or subject as well as a list of key authors and read-alikes.

Resources and techniques for keeping up-to-date and understanding new developments in the genre or subject are also provided. This section will not only aid staff already familiar with the genre or subject, but will also help those not familiar learn how to become so.

Tips for marketing collections and lists of resources and awards round out the tools staff need to be successful working with their community.

As readers who just happen to be readers' advisors, we hope that the guides in this series lead to longer to-be-read, -watched, and -listened-to piles. Our goal is that the series helps those new to RA feel supported and less at sea, and introduces new ideas or new ways of looking at foundational concepts, to advisors who have been at this a while. Most of all, we hope that this series helps advisors feel excited and eager to help patrons find their next great title. So dig in, explore, learn, and enjoy the almost alchemical process of connecting title and reader.

ACKNOWLEDGMENTS

I would like to deeply thank series editors Neal Wyatt and Joyce Saricks, both for their encouragement to write this book and for the endless ways they helped to make the final product better.

The RA community is a small world full of passionate people who inspire me every day. I want to thank all those with whom I have served in ALA for the joy you bring to the work of finding our patrons the perfect book. My Reading List colleagues in particular are treasured for the shared experience of reading our brains out and learning to really appreciate the great writing that can be found in every genre, even the ones you didn't think you liked! I would like to also thank early mentor Merle Jacob, who gave me a chance as a collection development librarian and set me on the readers' advisory path.

Finally, thanks to my husband for his love and support, as well as for his patience with the endless piles of books.

INTRODUCTION

WHAT IS GENRE BLENDING?

Genre is one of the most common ways that readers and those who serve them organize books. Within the larger category of fiction, most books can be identified by one genre label or another. If it isn't a label like "Mystery" or "Romance," it is a more amorphous label like "Literary Fiction" or "General Fiction." This label can be a physical one used by libraries, perhaps with a heart or a little cartoon of Sherlock Holmes; a label printed on the book cover by the publisher; or it can be a mental label that gets associated with a book because of the way the reader experiences the book. But those labels are only general guideposts to what might be between the covers. Every book offers a unique reading experience and has a narrative and a structure and a tone all its own. A growing number of books don't fit the traditional genre labels. If a book has some characteristics of one genre and some of another genre, what do you do with that book? Publishers have to decide how they will market that book and at what audience they will aim the mix. For readers, there are issues of discovery when a book exists in the borderlands between genres, and these *are* books that deserve to be discovered. As librarians, how do we make sure that readers will find genre blends in our collections? We need to figure out how to talk about genre blends with readers.

WHAT SHOULD WE CALL IT?

Call it genre blending, genre bending, genre crossover, hybrid fiction, literary mixing, or a mash-up. If you want to get formal and Latin, call it interstitial or liminal fiction. Some of the cool kids call it slipstream or the new weird. All these terms can be applied to books that do not sit neatly in one genre or category box, but combine elements of multiple genres or categories. Some terms, like *mash-up*, usually refer to books that take literature classics and mash them together with an unexpected genre (the popular book that arguably started the trend is Seth Grahame-Smith's *Pride and*

Prejudice and Zombies). These blends do of course play with genre, but in a satirical way with a sly wink. *Crossover* is a term applied in music for genre blending and is used for books that cross audiences (like YA books popular with adults) more than for those that cross genres. The *new weird* and *slipstream* are mostly limited to books that include an element of science fiction or fantasy. There is an inherent challenge in trying to come up with a name for books that by their nature defy easy categorization. Because I wanted to use a term that was broad and generously flexible, throughout this book I have defaulted to the term *genre blend*. By this I mean any book that combines two or more genres into one narrative.

THINKING ABOUT GENRE

Genre blending is not about breaking a genre or ignoring what makes it great—writers who blend must have a solid knowledge of and respect for a genre before they can use it. In other words, one has to know where the borders are to deliberately cross them. Genre is a way to group books that may provide a similar reading experience. The characteristics that books within a genre share can be plot related, as with mysteries or romances, or they can be setting based, as with historical fiction. Part of their definition can even be that they do not share characteristics with any genre, which is often what is meant when people use the term *literary fiction* as a genre. A reason people think about books in terms of genre is to have a shorthand that means "I liked this book, and this other book looks sort of like the book I liked." Genre is about expectations. Literature in general has to satisfy the reader's desire for the familiar and recognizable with the longing for something new and unexpected. Readers want to be surprised by what's new, different, and unique about a book and satisfied by how it met their expectations. The good thing about genre is that it can help lead readers to books that have characteristics they have enjoyed in the past. But librarians should keep in mind that genre is a nebulous concept that lots of people in the book publishing world and the book reading world have agreed upon (mostly) to help books find their readers. It is not a set of rules. If in individual chapters of this book I discuss the "formula" of a particular genre, please don't misunderstand. There is no one tried-and-true formula for any genre: add one part x, sprinkle in y, stir, and you get a genre best seller. Authors would be selling their souls for such a formula if it existed. But there are structures that some genres follow and attributes that they share.

Genre as a concept is created and supported by two separate but equally important groups, the first of which is the publishers who decide how to market a book, including decisions about things like what kind of cover to give it and what Book Industry Subject and Category subject headings (used by bookstores for shelving decisions) to assign to the book. But another group that cares about genre comprises the communities of readers who read and clamor for more of a particular storytelling style. Readers use genres (and subgenres) to find more of the stories they like. Where do authors fit into the mix? Well, authors certainly are the ones deciding what story to tell, but by and large I would doubt that many of them would care what label goes on their books as long as audiences find them. Some writers start their careers writing in a particular genre because those are the kinds of books they like to read. And some probably write in a genre because they think it is the path most likely to take them to a book contract. But most authors, I would say, simply have stories to tell. The way the stories manifest may end up sharing characteristics with a genre, but I would doubt that authors are obsessed with what genre their book is, as long as readers read it.

For the purposes of this work, I will be examining seven of the major genres used in publishing: adrenaline (a category used to cover adventure, thriller, and suspense), fantasy, historical fiction, horror, mystery, romance, and science fiction (SF). I chose these categories because they are some of the most clearly defined and remain recognizable even when blended with other genres. They are (with the addition of women's fiction) the categories used for judging the American Library Association's award for genre fiction, The Reading List. I have not covered women's fiction as it is less often found blended with other genres than the others, but some of the more romance-tending women's fiction titles have been folded into romance for the purposes of blending. I have also not included literary fiction, as it is mostly defined as a certain quality of writing (problematic for many reasons) and the absence of any other genre, although Appendix A tackles literary/genre blends.

THE PITFALLS OF GENRE

The problem with thinking of books as falling into only one genre—the one stamped on the cover—is that it's just too limiting. It leads people to not only believe that every book marketed under a certain genre heading is alike, but also that readers of this genre all like the same things.

There are so many other things that people read for besides genre. Readers might respond to a particular story line, such as a coming-of-age story, which can happen in any genre. They might be drawn to books with certain settings or situations, such as with exotic geographic settings or situations found in the urban lit category. There are readers who are character junkies, finding themselves drawn to stories that feature specific character types or wanting a certain kind of character development. Some readers also respond to certain styles of writing: lyrical descriptive prose, stream of consciousness, or stories moved primarily by dialogue. None of this can be captured by any one genre. Although some appeal characteristics might be more prevalent in one genre or another, the diligent readers' advisor can find them in every section of the library.

Genre is also not limiting enough. Within each and every genre are so many subgenres and variations in appeal characteristics, like tone or frame, that for a reader to say he likes a particular genre is just barely more helpful than him telling you he likes "good books." All librarians who work with readers have gotten that "good books" response, and just as in that situation, when someone only gives you a large genre as an answer to what kind of book they're looking for, you *must* delve deeper. Sometimes when a reader self-identifies as a fan of a particular genre she really does mean that she reads anything and everything in that genre, but usually a reader is looking for a certain kind of mystery or a particular subgenre of science fiction. The ability to narrow down a genre to a subgenre, and even to sub-subgenres can help zero in on what a reader is seeking, but without taking other appeal characteristics into account, genre—no matter how narrowly you slice it—will not get you there.

BOOKS ABOUT GENRE

In each chapter that follows, I try to give a very brief overview of one genre and its core appeals. Because the focus of each chapter is how that genre plays well with others, the analysis of each individual category is, out of necessity, limited. But there are some other great books that those seeking a more in-depth look at genre can turn to, and I highlight a few here.

One-stop Shopping

Joyce Saricks. 2009. *Readers' Advisory Guide to Genre Fiction.* 2nd edition. Chicago: American Library Association.

Saricks' book is a great primer for librarians thinking about genre. I utilize her groupings of genres into larger categories of Adrenaline, Emotional, Intellectual, and Landscape. She breaks down the appeal for each genre and will give anyone a good grounding in how to approach genre in our work with readers.

Cynthia Orr and Diana Tixier Herald. 2013. *Genreflecting: A Guide to Popular Reading Interests.* **Santa Barbara, California: Libraries Unlimited.**

This is the latest edition of a valuable and respected resource on genre.

Specific Genre Series

There are several long-running series that tackle specific genres. They all update their editions periodically.

ALA READERS' ADVISORY SERIES

Joyce Saricks and Neal Wyatt, eds. ALA Editions.

The series includes titles on mystery, science fiction, historical fiction, street literature, and graphic novels.

GENREFLECTING SERIES

Various eds. ABC-CLIO.

The series includes titles on all major fiction genres, a wide range of nonfiction areas, teen titles in fiction and nonfiction, graphic novels and manga, LGBT titles for adults and young adults, multicultural fiction, and urban fiction.

READ ON SERIES

Barry Trott, ed. Libraries Unlimited.

The series includes titles on crime, fantasy, science fiction, graphic novels, audiobooks, biography, teen speculative fiction, horror, historical fiction, women's fiction, and memoir.

WHY BLEND?

As I will explore in the chapters that follow, there are no genres that can't be combined. In fact, some genres have been blending so long that these blends have become subgenres of their own. Somewhere along the line, someone combined two genres, readers enjoyed the books and were willing to buy more books like them, and the blend became a category unto itself. Examples of blends that became their own subgenres are not hard to find, from large categories like historical mysteries to smaller ones like steampunk. These blends have accreted enough books that play off similar themes or elements that readers can find dozens (or hundreds) of books that deliver a similar reading experience.

Whether the blends are common or rare, each combination uses its genre elements in a new or unique way. A blended title can be the ideal book to give jaded readers who are sure they have explored everything your shelves have to offer. And these blends seem more popular than ever in recent years. The growth in genre blending is due to a lot of factors. One certainly is that a writer's sales (and a publisher's profits) no longer depend so completely on where a book is positioned in a store. Authors, whether explicitly or implicitly, are coached by agents and editors to make sure their books are marketable. That marketability often means the books need to fit in a category. But with the growth in smaller markets, self-publishing, and electronic discovery tools, the need to have a book ready-made for category marketing seems to be falling off.

Writers blend genres because they want to play with different narrative elements. Although there are writers who have spent much of their careers penning interstitial books that bridge various genres (see Appendix B for some blending MVPs), most start off in one genre. In writing a genre book, an author has both a tool kit of narrative elements to play with and a community of readers who love those narrative elements and are hungry for books that meet their genre expectations. What if writers like their narrative tool kit but long for one of the tools in a different genre's kit? Mystery writers, for example, have nearly infinite ways that they can tell a contemporary murder investigation narrative. But if they want, just for a change, to explore a historical setting or add a romance relationship arc, can they do this and still keep their mystery fans happy? The answer is a complicated "maybe." Some readers will follow a beloved author through any number of genre changes because they enjoy the way that author writes characters or his style or any other number of reasons. But there are readers who are not interested in anything outside of the narrative category they read regularly and enjoy. Writing is a deeply personal endeavor, and sometimes authors simply have to tell the stories they want to tell. It could be that the flexibility and empowerment available to fledgling writers to put out their own books without the need to satisfy the desire of publishers looking to round out their lists will mean that more genre-blended books will be available. If no one tells a writer that it is hard to promote a horror/romance or an SF/fantasy, will those and other blends that do not already have an established audience become more common? One can hope.

There are two things that writers need if they want to turn out a successful genre blend. One is a knowledge of and respect for both audience bases. If a writer is intentionally blending science fiction and romance, for example, she must not only turn in a believable, emotionally engaging story with a satisfying romantic resolution to engage with romance fans, but must also feed the needs of the science fiction fan who requires believable science. Reading a few romances and throwing in some techno-jargon will not work for either fan base. The other thing the author needs in order to have a blend truly work is a real *love* of the genres being used. If the genre is being used ironically or is thrown in for variety, it is not going to work well as a blend. Readers will know.

MARKETING BLENDS

It's probably a good idea to keep in mind that the book business *is a business*. Genre fiction came into being because it made publishing more predictable and thereby more profitable as publishers could market books like commodities to a specific audience (Smith 2004). And when writers create works that don't look like the commodities that readers are used to consuming, what's a publisher to do? I'm sure there have been many blendy, bendy genre books that have been turned down because they are deemed too difficult to market. The decision of what category or genre to put a book in is still mainly the decision of the book's publisher. Sometimes books with very clear genre characteristics are not marketed as such because the publisher believes the book will find more readers without a genre label on the spine. Authors whose books are often stealthy genre titles include Margaret Atwood, Jonathan Lethem, Kurt Vonnegut, Kate Atkinson, Justin Cronin, and Michael Chabon. Chabon has, in fact, written extensively about his love for genre, but literary fiction has claimed him as its own and so his books are not marketed as genre (Chabon 2008).

Marketing decisions get remarkably complicated when a book blends genres. On the one hand it would seem like a win-win proposition for publishers: they get fans of both genres to buy the book, right? Well . . . sometimes. But sometimes, in an unfortunate Boolean turn of events, instead of ending up with a book that has an audience that includes people who read x genre *or* people who read y genre, you find yourself with a book that only appeals to people who read both x *and* y genres. If instead of trying to find that intersection of fan bases a publisher decides to push a book as one of its genres rather than another, will readers respond? Will the added zest of a blended genre attract new readers or alienate those expecting a "regular" genre book? How do you decide which genre to stress? This last question might be especially difficult. If a genre-blended book is by its nature more than one genre, the decision of whether to pick one or another of its elements to hang a marketing campaign upon is a tricky one for publishers. These decisions will determine things like the cover art used, the blurbs and promotional copy on the book, and the way the publisher pitches the book to reviewers and book buyers. All of these factors have a huge impact on who is likely to find the book and decide to read it.

For some genre-blended books, the author has chosen to stress one genre more than another and that becomes the genre that is given more weight in marketing decisions. But when a book really has multiple genres mixed together somewhat evenly, how do publishers determine how to promote it? An author's prominence in one of the blended genres might be the deciding factor, as he might have a built-in fan base for the publisher to market to. For example, when thriller writer Michael Koryta started writing fabulous blended thriller/horror books such as *So Cold the River*, his stature in the thriller field meant that that book and the other equally spooky ones he wrote afterward got cover treatments and marketing strategies aimed at thriller fans. Sometimes the issue is avoided altogether by *not* promoting the book as a genre at all—leave it in general fiction and hope readers find it. The recent time travel books *Blackout* and *All Clear* by SF author Connie Willis are a good example of this. The covers stress the historical fiction elements, with stark black-and-white photography and plain backgrounds. Contrast with early editions of her first book in the same series (1992's *The Doomsday Book*), which had a much more genre look about it with a woman in a cloak and a futuristic car in the background. The books in this series have found an audience beyond genre, and the publisher wants to be sure that even those who don't read SF would not hesitate to pick up the new titles. Sometimes the genre that is perceived by the publisher to be the higher prestige genre will be stressed for marketing purposes. For example, Justin Cronin's *The Passage* is a mix of horror, science fiction, and thriller, but the publisher has carefully chosen a cover and blurbs that will entice thriller readers, and while not hiding the fact that there are supernatural elements to the story, certainly plays them down.

With some blended books, the books end up promoted as one genre over the other because of issues of dominance. There are simply some genres that take over a book when they are mixed in. Perhaps not narratively (although sometimes there too), but in the perception of who will be interested in reading it. A genre like science fiction is very versatile for blending, but the resulting books almost always read like SF. Another classic example is romance. Add a romantic plotline to any other genre and it almost always gets marketed as a romance. The exceptions are if the author is a man (Nicholas Sparks, I'm looking at you), or if the author has a strong reputation in another genre or in the literary fiction crowd. Otherwise, romances mixed-in with other genres end up promoted as subgenres of the romance category (i.e., historical romance, SF romance, paranormal romance, romantic suspense) and the books are seen as suitable only for women. This doesn't have to be a bad thing—the romance market is robust and strong selling and is by no means a bad place for an author to be positioned—but it does mean that some readers who might otherwise have read and enjoyed a book will now not be willing to pick it up. The marketing of romances, which is effective in the sense of making it clear that a book *is* a romance, can be off-putting for some readers. The cover art can be cheesy, with scantily clad men and women with flowing hair and pouting lips. The format is often mass market paperback (helping to make the books seem like ephemera to be read and discarded). They are also rarely reviewed outside of library publications, which also signals that they are not considered real literature. This means that authors that write books that blend in dominant genres like romance often must resign themselves to having that genre take over the marketing of their books.

LIBRARY ISSUES

Libraries and Genre

Librarians love genre, because it gives us a handle to put on a book. We are organizers, categorizers, and in general people who like to know the proper place for everything in our collections. One big controversy in the admittedly small world of readers' advisory is whether our collections should have separate sections for genre, or whether they should all be shelved together. On one side is the argument that separating genre serves readers, allowing them to browse only the books that they are interested in (Baker 2002). On the other side are those that believe that keeping everything together allows for greater serendipitous discovery. Whether a library separates or does not separate any of the standard genres, librarians definitely spend time thinking about genre, assigning subject headings, and applying stickers. We use genre to help narrow the universe of offerings in our buildings and our online catalogs to a manageable subset. This is meant to help those who like to browse our collections and discover quickly and easily the books they like best. Talking about books in terms of their genre is not a bad place to start a readers' advisory conversation. It can help a readers' advisor know what direction to begin a search. Discussion and further narrowing of genre to subgenre might be a perfectly effective way to get at some readers' book needs. But in libraries, and whenever people are thinking about books and reading, genre cannot be everything.

How Do Libraries Deal with Genre Blends?

If libraries are conflicted in how we deal with genre, how much more complicated does it get when a book blends more than one genre? How does a library catalog that book? Does it get one genre sticker or more than one? Where does the library shelve the book if it usually separates genre? How do we as librarians promote the book? All of these questions interest me but it is the last question of how we get these blends into the right person's hands that made me want to write this readers' advisory guide.

The physical handling of the books is tricky, as you want the readers who will enjoy the book to be able to find it. In an ideal world, for a book that blended science fiction and romance, a library could have one copy in SF and one in romance. But most libraries don't have the time or money (or the inclination) to shelve books in more than one location. This means the library must choose a location. Sometimes the librarian who selected the book might guide that decision, but usually other staff handles decisions about genre. This might be technical services staff if a library catalogs its own materials, or it might be a vendor who supplies the book that makes the call. Both groups rely on information provided from the publisher to make their decision about genre categorization. A librarian can override those decisions if she thinks a publisher's choices will not necessarily find the appropriate audience, but let's be honest—who's got that kind of time? Unless a staff person or a reader comes back to us asking for a reclassification of the book, we are right back to depending on the marketing choices of the publishing house for how we position a book in our collection.

The beautiful thing about the improvements being made in online catalogs for our collections is that they are now most patrons' preferred way to navigate our holdings. Not that physical browsing is by any means dead, but with the growth of online browsing and e-books, it behooves libraries to make the most of the online discovery tools at our disposal. Subject headings for fiction are a fairly recent invention (compared to nonfiction subject headings) and are not used by every library. Even when they are used, they have limitations in how they present genre. A check of one library catalog (which does use fiction subject headings) for several popular urban fantasy series shows that none of them use the terms "Urban Fantasy;" most only use "Fantasy Fiction" and to confuse things even more, one uses "Fantastic Fiction" instead. Unlike Library of Congress subject headings for nonfiction which are fairly standardized (if not perfect by any means), the ones used for fiction are much more variable. This means that even across one library you can have trouble linking together similar books if you rely of subject heading alone. But some new catalogs also allow local creation of tags and taxonomies as well as storing and displaying librarian-created booklists that all serve to supplement the standard bibliographic record. Some libraries are also using third-party RA products like Novelist to help readers discover readalikes on their own. I strongly encourage libraries, even those with strong fiction subject access in their catalogs, to do everything they can to take advantage of local tagging, online booklists, and other catalog and website tools to help your readers find those books that don't fit neatly into genre boxes.

If the online catalog can only imperfectly help those who want to find genre blends, how can libraries increase the chances that readers will find the blended books in our collections? The answer is librarians, of course. Through displays and booklists, hand selling, and RA interviewing, we are the ones who can make sure that these books find their readers and don't get lost on our shelves. Chapter 9 covers the interesting challenges of readers' advisory for genre-blended books.

FORMAT OF THE BOOK

As you will see, this book is organized into seven major genres. For each genre, I have started with a brief description of the genre and its most common appeal characteristics. I add a section on why the genre gets blended, which tries to be a bit on both why a writer might blend with it and why a reader might want a book with this genre in a blend. Next are separate sections for that genre's blends with the other six genres. Deciding which books to include in each chapter was sometimes a difficult task. This difficulty sometimes came because there were not a lot of books out there that combined the two genres. Sometimes it was hard to choose only three titles because there were so many books with a particular blend. And sometimes it was a matter of choosing in which chapter a book best fit. I considered this my Crayola crayon problem. Remember the "yellow-orange" and "orange-yellow" crayons? It was really hard to tell the difference between the two, wasn't it? Well, some of these blends are really successful in the way they combine genres, to the point where deciding whether something was more of a historical/mystery blend or a mystery/historical blend became very difficult. Just as with the crayons, though, the distinction usually became clear when you held the two side by side. When choosing where to highlight a book, I used my own judgment of which fan base I thought would reach for a book first. Finally, for every highlighted blend, I tried to give reading paths. Not just readalikes (although often they could work as those as well), these suggestions are meant to give someone who read a book a sense of what books could be paths back to the genres that were combined. So for an adrenaline/fantasy blend, I suggest one title that might be a good fit for someone who liked the book but wanted more adrenaline, and one title for someone who wanted more of a fantasy. Finally, each chapter ends with some brief tips on working with that genre's blends.

1

ADRENALINE BLENDS
Blends on the Edge of Your Seat

Fast-paced. Pulse pounding. Nerve wracking. Page turning. Action packed. These are all words that describe a particular kind of reading experience. The genres that Joyce Saricks has grouped under the umbrella of adrenaline belong together because they share that experience (Saricks 2009). If you read a book and find you cannot put it down, there could be a lot of reasons for this such as great characters, gorgeous language, and so on. But often a big reason books are called page-turners comes down to plot and pacing. If you need to keep reading because you simply can't wait to find out what happens next, there is a good chance that you are reading an adrenaline book. This category of books includes the genres of thriller, adventure, and suspense. Tension-filled books that are very plot dependent characterize all these genres. Thrillers are a hugely popular genre, making up a good chunk of the *New York Times* best-seller list each week. They are action packed, have clear good guy/bad guy dichotomies, and usually have an interesting background frame. They often involve crime but have more of a focus on stopping a bad guy rather than figuring out who the bad guy is. Adventure is very similar to thrillers but with even more of an emphasis on the frame. They usually involve exotic locales and over-the-top action. Adventure books are very "mission" oriented, have that same moral dichotomy of good guy/bad guy, and often have military (or former military) characters, action, and jargon. Suspense usually shares a criminal element with thrillers, but they are usually smaller scaled. They are less likely to have the clear black-and-white morality common in adventure and thriller. The cast of characters is often smaller, and the pacing is based on building psychological tension rather than the more physical adrenaline of thrillers and adventure.

An adrenaline read grabs you with an intriguing premise or setup and then is constructed, quite carefully and deliberately, to make you *need* to keep reading all the way to the satisfying climax. It doesn't have to be nonstop action. Although many of the books under this umbrella are full of things happening one after the other so that you are pulled inexorably through the story, this doesn't necessarily translate into car chases and gun battles. It can simply be a buildup of anticipation and tension. This is usually how the suspense titles earn their adrenaline reputation. With books labeled as thriller and adventure, the adrenaline rush is often caused by a combination of internal tension and external action, and they often have high stakes and big, action-filled climaxes. For suspense, the adrenaline just as often comes from a psychological source and, while there may still be physical danger, the scale is smaller—one protagonist in danger rather than thousands of people in mortal peril. Whether bad guys or inner demons are chasing you, though, a successful adrenaline read relies on building tension to a big finish.

APPEAL OF ADRENALINE

Some people read books to learn more about the human condition and like to see their own experiences reflected in the books they read. Adrenaline titles, like most other genre fiction, are less about seeing your life exactly mirrored in literature and more about having a vicarious experience. This is not to say that genre fiction in general and adrenaline reads in particular do not speak to us about our own lives, but they do so more in a metaphorical sense. A reader may not go on continent-hopping hunts for super villains or get chased by axe-wielding serial killers, but a skilled writer of adrenaline can usually find a way to examine how society and human beings behave in heightened circumstances. People enjoy adrenaline books the same way they like to read travel books about places they have no intention of visiting: it's good to live vicariously through books sometimes. While there are books that you read and think, I wish that would happen to me! that is usually not the case with this genre. Sure, there might be some wish-fulfillment aspects to an adrenaline read. For example, with adventure books (and some thrillers as well) it might be nice to imagine traveling to their settings in exotic places, but read on and you quite often find that the exotic place is fraught with danger. Usually, adrenaline reads involve things happening to characters that would be a reader's worst nightmare—murder, mayhem, and cataclysmic disasters are just a sample of what might be inflicted on an adrenaline hero or heroine. But just like with mystery, the climax of all that action is usually a very satisfying resolution. The bad guy gets punished, the world is saved, and folks are able to go back to their normal lives. We all like to believe that we would behave well in a crisis but hope that we never have to prove it. In adrenaline reads, we get to watch other people deal with the bad stuff, and (usually) have the reward of seeing them come out the other side.

WHY BLEND?

As much fun as an adrenaline read can be, a steady diet of nothing but adrenaline could leave a reader pretty shaky. Even those who live for thrillers, die for adventure, and can't wait for their next suspense read might want to add some variety. Variety could come by way of a step next door to a genre like mystery, which shares a lot of readers with adrenaline. But if a reader is looking for high-octane action and tense standoffs and doesn't mind a shift in scenery, whole aisles of the library can open up. Some readers don't think they could ever like adrenaline titles because they are too intense or too grisly. A blend can be a way to try out an adrenaline genre but still have the trappings of a genre with which they are more comfortable. The part of the adrenaline genre that most often carries through to any blend is the pacing, and that can be of great benefit to any genre. Genres normally known for slower pacing, such as the landscape genres fantasy and historical fiction, have a completely different feel when blended with adrenaline. You might still have gorgeous world building, but if you borrow from thrillers and adventure, the landscape might just whiz by. The pacing is not just fast, but it's about building and accelerating tension, making adrenaline blends often just as hard to put down as the unblended variety. At its heart adrenaline is the *danger* genre, and any story could benefit from a touch of danger.

THE BLENDS

Adrenaline/Fantasy

Adrenaline books are often known just as much for their interesting frame as their compelling pacing. This emphasis on frame can make adrenaline a great blend with fantasy, a genre all about building fascinating worlds.

With the accelerating tension of adrenaline reads, the goal is often to keep the reader off-balance and on edge. Again, adding the weirdness and otherness of fantasy can add to the effect. The fantasy genre has a lot of variety under its umbrella and can therefore appeal to many different kinds of readers, but it is usually thought of as a more leisurely read. Finding fast-paced fantasy is a lot easier than it used to be with the explosion of urban fantasy and its crime-solving plots, and this chapter's challenge became finding things that showcase the imagination and worlds of fantasy but could still be handed to a reader more comfortable with thrillers or suspense. The easiest way to find these blends is to start with an adrenaline based on a real-world action or adventure plot that happens to have a supernatural or fantastic twist. This twist can lend a subtle otherness to the plot or it can be a game-change paradigm shift, depending on the blend. Perhaps because of the dark edge that a lot of adrenaline books have, blends between adrenaline also tend to lean more heavily toward the dark fantasy end of things. Fantasy can make an already high-stakes genre like adrenaline even more intense, as magical threats make even serial killers and terrorists seem manageable. By not having the full immersion into the made-up world common in epic fantasy, readers not used to that kind of world building will have an easier time getting into the story. Less world building also allows for the fast-paced narrative that epitomizes adrenaline. Instead of having to spend a lot of time describing the scenery, clothes, social structure, and so on, the author can plunge readers right into the action and interweave the fantastic elements without slowing down the plot. The fantasy in an adrenaline/fantasy blend can be our world with just one or two things different. But those one or two things, once known by the protagonist and shown to the reader, can change everything.

Lexicon by **Max Barry**

Words have power. It's a common saying, but what if that were actually true? A secretive group that trains "poets" to use language to compel or even kill others is at the heart of this breakneck thriller. The story kicks off with a bang when Wil Parke is jumped at the airport, his girlfriend is killed in front of him, and he is forced to help two men who think he is the key to stopping a devastating catastrophe. Another interwoven story tells us about a young recruit to the poets who cons her way into the school that trains those with potential to learn how to collect and apply words that will allow a poet to control another person. How these stories intersect is part of the gripping action-packed narrative. The suspense is created and maintained quite cleverly, as Barry only lets the reader know things when they will land with the greatest effect. Chases, explosions, and a race toward a cataclysmic climax makes this a book that readers will tear through, but the linguistic magic system and world of the poets is so interesting that those same readers won't want the book to end. The poets seem like wizards, but there is enough logic to the explanation of how they are trained to use language as a weapon that science fiction fans could be easily handed *Lexicon* as well.

READING PATHS

If you like the word-centric plot and want a thriller:

Codex by Lev Grossman

If you like the magic system, where words have power, and want fantasy:

The Name of the Wind by Patrick Rothfuss

The Traveler by John Twelve Hawks (FOURTH REALM TRILOGY, BOOK 1)

Rival secret societies battle for control of the world in this intriguing blend of geo-political thriller and fantasy. The Tabula, a society that secretly controls the world, has targeted two brothers. Although they don't know it, the two are Travelers, members of the society that opposes the Tabula. The Travelers have mystical abilities to send their spirits out of their bodies into other dimensions, and they are almost extinct in the world. Protecting them are warriors known as Harlequins, and Maya is one such warrior who must keep the brothers out of Tabula hands. It takes longer to describe the world in this rocketing thriller than it does to experience it, since pseudonymous author Hawks throws readers right into the action. The combination of technology and magic is tricky, but it's handled here by giving us enough of an idea why the Travelers and their powers are important and then focusing on the thriller plot to keep them safe from the evil Tabula forces. It will resonate most with those open to a new-agey philosophy and a healthy tolerance for conspiracy theories, and it is undoubtedly quite a ride. The author's actual identity is unknown and his bio states that he lives completely off the grid.

READING PATHS

If you like secret society action and want more of a thriller:

Angels & Demons by Dan Brown

If you like secret powers that control the world and want more fantasy:

Angelology by Danielle Trussoni

Declare by Tim Powers

There have been fantasy novels that posit a super-secret spy agency involved with the supernatural, but the espionage subgenre is often used almost as a cliché. In *Declare*, Powers plays the spy craft absolutely straight. We get the story of young Andrew Hale, recruited onto the British Secret Service rolls as a child but not called up until WWII to serve his country. Hale is studying at Oxford in 1941, and before he really knows what's happening, his handler has arranged that he be arrested by the British, recruited by the Soviets, and sent deep undercover to Paris for his initiation in the Great Game of espionage. The defining mission of Hale's career is Operation Declare, under which in 1948 and again in 1963 the British and Soviets fought to control a supernatural power hidden on Mount Ararat. This is a challenging work with intricate plotting, shifts back and forward in time, and spies who are turned and turned again as their loyalties and politics change with the wind. The period details, including all the convoluted spy craft, are meticulously researched and supported with real-life historical personages like famed British spy Kim Philby to give added depth. Hale's work for a secret and oft-disavowed section of British intelligence leads him into some pretty tense and dangerous situations, and his loyalties only become more complicated by his love for a female spy he met on his first assignment in Paris. The supernatural dangers in *Declare* are very real, very old, and very scary, especially in the big showdown back on Mount Ararat, but it is the well-crafted spy drama that will impress readers.

READING PATHS

If you like the double agents and deep cover and want a more serious thriller:

Tinker, Tailor, Soldier, Spy by John Le Carré

If you like the Cold War espionage and want a fantasy:

Babayaga by Toby Barlow

Adrenaline/Historical Fiction

There is a key reason that authors choose a historical setting for an adrenaline story. Although the action of an adrenaline book can just as easily happen in an unknown town in the present day, the tradition of utilizing exotic settings is a strong one in thrillers and adventure novels. Adding another dimension of a time period removed from our own gives these blends another level of exoticism, which is very appealing to some readers. No matter what decade or century, what city or region, the setting has been chosen because it's an *interesting* time in which to imagine living. Not necessarily comfortable, but interesting! And the things that drive interest are usually great fodder for adrenaline reads: war, unrest, social upheaval, political turmoil, and so on. One of the ways to enhance the exoticism so popular with adrenaline readers and also with historical fiction fans is to set a book in a time and place that people feel like they don't already know everything about. Although there are certainly always people ready to read another Tudor book, the lesser-visited settings are rewarding for readers because they feel like they learn something and experience something totally different and totally new. A classic plot in adrenaline reads is to have the main character go up against impossible odds. The historical setting can make that kind of plot even more interesting, and sometimes even more believable. How much harder must it be for adrenaline authors to find ways to keep their characters in danger in the modern age when help can be summoned through a cell phone? Adding a historical setting to adrenaline plots ups the danger quotient, throws obstacles at the characters and in general makes everything more difficult—all good things for creating a suspenseful, tension-filled read.

Labyrinth by Kate Mosse (Languedoc, book 1)

While volunteering at an archaeological dig in the south of France, American Alice Tanner finds the skeletal remains of two people in a hidden cave that is engraved with an intricate labyrinth. This discovery involves her in a centuries-old hunt for three missing books that might hold the secret to the famous Holy Grail. Her story is twinned with that of a woman who lived 800 years earlier in the medieval town of Carcasonne and who was also connected to the books and their secrets. We alternate between modern Alice and medieval Alaïs, and both stories are full of action, adventure, betrayal, and intrigue—plus a lot of fun racing around to protect books. But the medieval story is what sets this apart from many *Da Vinci Code* imitators that filled the shelves for years after that title hit so big. Mosse has a real feel for the history of the region and its unique language and heritage, and the resonance of Alice's and Alaïs stories adds depth to this historical thriller. The modern story will also ease the way for those who aren't normally big readers of historical fiction.

READING PATHS

If you like the bibliocentric grail story and want a thriller:

The Da Vinci Code by Dan Brown

If you liked the history of the Cathars in Southern France and want historical fiction:

The Treasure of Montsegur by Sophy Burnham

Child 44 by Tom Rob Smith (LEO DEMIDOV, BOOK 1)

Although there has been historical fiction set in Russia, using this setting during the Soviet era is less common. In this series, beginning with *Child 44*, Smith brings us to the bad old days of the Stalinist period of Soviet history. The party line (literally!) in 1950s Russia is that crime does not exist because the state takes care of everyone. Leo Demidov is a state security officer, rounding up people who commit the only acknowledged crimes left: those against the state itself. After he gets caught up in internal departmental politics, Leo is exiled to the countryside, where he starts to see a pattern of child murders that looks like the work of a serial killer. Investigating such a thing is dangerous in Stalin's Russia, but the brutal nature of the killings means that Leo cannot bring himself to look away. The pacing here is relentless, with Leo facing obstacles everywhere he turns. Smith doesn't shy away from any reader's tender sensibilities, and the crimes are described in quite graphic detail, made more awful because of the age of the victims. But the horrific details and child victims also raise the stakes and compel both Leo and the reader to be desperate for a resolution.

READING PATHS

If you like the Russian setting and want a more modern thriller:

Gorky Park by Martin Cruz Smith

If you like the chilling portrayal of Stalin-era Russia and want historical fiction:

The Betrayal by Helen Dunmore

The Alienist by Caleb Carr (LASZLO KREIZLER, BOOK 1)

The thriller staple of a serial killer may seem like a modern malady, but one of the most famous killers in history, Jack the Ripper, operated at the turn of the 19th century. That case surely inspired Caleb Carr's historical thriller, set in 1896, just eight years after the Ripper was active. Also involving the brutal slaying of prostitutes, the murder investigation in *The Alienist* is kicked off by none other than Teddy Roosevelt, who was then commissioner of the New York City Police Department (NYPD). Fearing corruption in his own police force, Roosevelt recruits two outsiders—a reporter and a psychologist (an "alienist" in the parlance of the day) to help find the killer. The crimes are particularly heinous, as the victims were mere children, young boys who dressed as girls and sold themselves for money. As reporter Moore hits the streets and alienist Kreizler builds a criminal profile, we get a vivid picture of not only the dawn of forensic investigation techniques, but also a gritty picture of New York City. The limited tools available to these investigators, as well as the corruption and political machinations of the time, add suspense to the narrative.

READING PATHS

If you want another look at the early days of detective work and want a thriller:

Murder as a Fine Art by David Morrell

If you like the New York setting and want historical fiction:

The Tea Rose by Jennifer Donnelly

Adrenaline/Horror

Both adrenaline and horror are about building tension and making you nervous. In both genres, for a book to resonate, readers need to be invested in the characters so that they care about their fate and wince at every horrible thing the writer puts them through. Where the two genres diverge is often in the details. An adrenaline book from the adventure or thriller end of things will probably be much higher in action: breakneck races through foreign alleyways; races against the clock or the killer; car chases and gunfights galore. The pacing accelerates, building and building to a big finish. You can inject horror into these thriller and adventure plots, but it's not horror's usual modus operandi. Horror wants to creep up on you, jump out and scare you, back away so you think you are safe, and then scare you again. Blends with horror and thriller or horror and adventure will usually adopt the general arc of adrenaline pacing but borrow horror's monsters and use its sudden jolts of scary intensity to make the pacing even more nerve racking.

The suspense genre within adrenaline is an even closer kin to horror, as both genres expertly manipulate mood and atmosphere to build tension. Whereas the action-based genres of thriller and adventure want to propel readers through rapidly accelerating events so that they barely have time to think about what's happening because the story is racing along, horror and suspense both want you to have time to think about and dread what's coming. Those pauses or slower passages in the pacing are valuable breathing space, but they also increase the menacing air and tension because the reader knows that the bad thing (supernatural or human) is still out there waiting. The other interesting thing blending adrenaline and horror together can bring is that the ending can be more uncertain. Whereas with the adrenaline genres there is usually a satisfying and tidy ending, horror is much more likely to leave evil unvanquished and bad things lurking and waiting for the next poor guy. When you blend, you just don't know what kind of ending you might get.

The Passage by **Justin Cronin (PASSAGE, BOOK 1)**

Vampires are one of the oldest and greatest horror monsters. Although there have been some vampire books that attempt to give them an origin myth, most leave the source of vampirism in the distant past and out of the story. Cronin takes an entirely different approach and one that works especially well for a thriller, which is to have his revenants be the result of lab experiment gone wrong. In the near future, the US government attempts to create a super-strong, nearly immortal soldier but accidentally unleashes a viral plague that turns people into bloodsucking monsters. Jump forward a hundred years and the remnants of humanity are barricaded in compounds and on the brink of extinction. Their hope for survival centers on Amy, a very unusual six-year-old girl. Just because these vampires originated in a petri dish and not in the mountains of Transylvania doesn't make them any less scary. In fact, those less interested in the supernatural will probably find them even *more* terrifying for being vaguely possible. The carnage of the "virals" and beleaguered state of the small number of survivors will be just what horror fans are looking for, and those tired of vampires that sparkle and flirt will celebrate the return of the evil blood-drinking monster. The structure and setup are just as appealing for thriller readers, with some great bio-thriller intrigue at the lab and then gripping survival action when we jump forward. The descriptions of future life in the compounds (bonus SF genre!) are a vivid detailing of the new shape of this society. Just like with Stephen King's *The Stand* (which will be an obvious readalike), the massive length seems like it flies by, with no wasted scenes or filler. It's action and blood and humans in peril, and I dare you to put it down.

READING PATHS

If you like the classic monster that's brewed up in the lab and want a thriller:

The Strain by Guillermo del Toro and Chuck Hogan

If you like the apocalyptic setting and want horror:

Sparrow Rock by Nate Kenyon

Relic by Douglas Preston and Lincoln Child (PENDERGAST, BOOK 1)

Horror often relies on the thing that lurks in the dark and strikes without warning, which works especially well when paired with the structure and pacing of a thriller, as in *Relic*. Deep in the bowels of New York City's Natural History Museum are crates shipped back from an expedition to the Amazon that ended with the death of all involved. The museum is preparing for a special exhibition about native superstitions and plans to use a figurine from that Amazonian haul as a highlight. But during preparations for the exhibit opening, people start dying at the museum, eviscerated by a creature that should not exist. Graduate student Margo Green finds herself at the center of the hunt for a way to stop the creature, aided by odd but oddly compelling FBI agent Pendergast. Thrillers often employ exotic settings, and the museum is a fantastic case of a seemingly mundane city institution that once explored is plenty exotic (and more than a little scary).

The huge size and labyrinthine nature of the museum are used to great effect as the book races to its gore-filled and action-packed conclusion, with visitors and dignitaries trapped and the creature picking them off a few at a time. The investigation of the nature of the creature will satisfy those who like bio-thrillers, delving into anthropology, evolution, and genetics. But Green and Pendergast's race through the spooky corridors of the museum to stop the carnage is what will keep readers turning pages.

READING PATHS

If you like the tense atmosphere and unique setting and want a thriller:

Amazonia by James Rollins

If you like the creature from the jungle hunting humanity and want more horror:

Castaways by Brian Keene

Hater by David Moody (HATER, BOOK 1)

Danny has a dead-end job in the parking enforcement office and three kids under 10, and there's never enough money or time to do anything but barely keep his head above water. One day outside his office he witnesses a random and brutal attack when a man stabs an elderly woman in the stomach, seemingly without reason or provocation. This is just the first of many strange occurrences of violence that are occurring all over Britain. At first people believe that it is just an uptick in violent crime, but soon it appears to be more of an epidemic, with the attackers dubbed "Haters" by the media. The author uses the extremely effective technique of opening each chapter with one of these attacks, as seen from the point of view of the attacker. In each case, the person suddenly and with no warning turns to the person nearest them and seems to be overcome by the unshakable knowledge that this person is going to try to kill them. What could be more natural than to kill them first? Chilling and unnerving as the logical nature of the Haters' point of view is, Moody doesn't stint on the gory details of the attacks. The foreboding that builds as the incidents seem to accelerate and the unknown origin of the Hater epidemic give this work a great narrative tension. It's a zombie epidemic without the zombies but with that same "us versus them" framework and the sense that anyone could turn. The book, which was self-published online before being picked up by one of the big boys, is the first in the series, so those who hate cliffhangers, fair warning.

READING PATHS

If you like the plot of society facing an epidemic and want a thriller:

Cell by Stephen King

If you like the tense zombie action and want horror:

The Walking by Bentley Little

Adrenaline/Mystery

What flips a mystery into adrenaline territory? There is a certain level of tension and suspense in most mysteries, as the reader has to care about catching the killer. But that tension can be pretty muted in cozy mysteries and the more genteel puzzle plots. The more action-packed or suspenseful a mystery is, the harder it gets to tell whether it is more mystery or adrenaline. And really, it doesn't matter. As long as readers can find the balance they are looking for, the genre label that gets printed on the cover is irrelevant. The adrenaline stories that are most easily blended with mystery are those that involve an investigator trying to stop a killer. Because adrenaline stories are often just a little bigger than other genres, the killings tend to be bigger too, and the stakes higher. Serial killers have long been a staple of the thriller genre in particular. These stories are more chilling than a one-and-done murder because there is the implied threat that the killer here will go on killing until he is caught and the lack of any motive beyond homicidal psychopathy adds a special level of anxiety to a book. Mystery readers can be attracted to these stories because they do contain at their heart a crime-and-punishment story. The different storytelling techniques may or may not click with mystery readers, however, as the narrative has often changed with the serial killer story to more of a chase than an investigation. To appeal to those drawn more to mysteries, there has to be at least some searching for clues and not all running around after the killer. Mysteries are much more intent on hiding the identity of the killer from readers until the big reveal at the end. The blends that work best for mystery fans will keep the killer's identity unknown and keep that investigation piece in the story, saving the high-octane chases for the end. But the body count doesn't have to be in the double digits to be an adrenaline read. Suspense/mystery blends can be just as successful, but there the scale tends to go the other direction—one killer, one victim, and more of a cat-and-mouse dynamic to ratchet up the tension. The suspense-based blends with mystery are less likely to have professional investigators, such as from law enforcement, because they have too many tools to catch killers and part of the suspense often comes from the tension of a potential victim as underdog against superior forces. Whatever the adrenaline base for a mystery blend, the shelves have plenty of options for readers.

The Girl with the Dragon Tattoo by Stieg Larsson (MILLENNIUM, BOOK 1)

This blockbuster series from Larsson begins with disgraced journalist Mikael Blomkvist getting called out to a remote island in Northern Sweden to meet with powerful businessman Henrik Vanger who wants to hire Mikael to find out what happened to his granddaughter. Harriet Vanger disappeared without a trace 40 years ago, and Henrik will give Mikael the evidence he needs to nail the man who caused his journalistic downfall if he agrees to look into the old mystery. Assisting him is one of the most amazing fictional constructions of recent years, the damaged but indomitable hacker Lisbeth Salander. As the two investigate the many suspicious members of the Vanger family, we get a unique combination of financial thriller and locked-room mystery. The remote nature of the family compound where the crime took place means that there is a very small pool of family members who could have killed Harriet, and the tension escalates as it becomes clear that the killer will eliminate anyone who gets too close, including Mikael and Lisbeth.

READING PATHS

If you like the Nordic setting and dark tone and want a thriller:

The Snowman by Jo Nesbo

If you like the damaged but brilliant investigator and want a mystery:

Mallory's Oracle by Carol O'Connell

Gone Girl by Gillian Flynn

Flynn found an interesting way to blend mystery and suspense by having her twisty, dark story start out as a mystery and then change midway through into psychological suspense. Amy Dunne disappears on her fifth wedding anniversary, and the narrative initially seems like it will follow the mystery path as the reader tries to find out who might have wanted to kill her. The spouse is always a suspect, and Amy's husband Nick does seem to have a lot of secrets. By alternating chapters from Nick's point of view with excerpts from Amy's diaries, Flynn gives us a story of a wife afraid of her husband, and it seems obvious why the police target Nick as their prime suspect. Just when the reader thinks he has the narrative mapped out, though, Flynn takes a fascinating turn. Dread and suspense are present throughout but kick into high gear to give readers a cat-and-mouse second act that is utterly gripping and twisted. By turning the expectations of a mystery upside down, Flynn opens up new avenues for her narrative, which becomes both a fascinatingly dark look at marriage as well as a creepy character study.

READING PATHS

If you like the question of whether a crime has been committed and want more psychological suspense:

The Dead Lie Down by Sophie Hannah

If you like the moody atmosphere and want a dark mystery:

Garnethill by Denise Mina

Rules of Prey by John Sandford (PREY, BOOK 1)

Look at the Prey series in libraries around the country and it becomes obvious that there is a split about whether or not to put these books under mystery or thriller. On the one hand, they are police procedurals (usually considered mysteries) by virtue of their series investigator Lucas Davenport. But the plots, including that of this first volume, tend to be fast-paced, violent, serial-killer chases, which are often found in thrillers. Both fan bases can easily enjoy the series, so it doesn't really matter what label goes on the spine. The theme of *Rules of Prey* is games, both the ones that cop Davenport codes in his spare time and the sick game set up by a serial killer who wants to be known as "maddog." As the rapist/killer takes each victim, he leaves behind rules that guide his killings to taunt the police, and tension mounts steadily in a cat-and-mouse contest. The killer's identity and double life are revealed early on, eliminating the puzzle piece that most mystery lovers enjoy, but keeping the law enforcement hero will ensure crossover appeal.

READING PATHS

If you like serial killers leading double lives and want a thriller:

Pop Goes the Weasel by James Patterson

If you like the dark psychological police procedural and want a mystery:

The Neon Rain by James Lee Burke

Adrenaline/Romance

Most of the books that combine adrenaline and romance fall under the genre of romantic suspense and are read by women. Women are also overwhelmingly the ones writing romantic suspense, the covers are markedly different than their thriller cousins, and they focus a lot of their narrative energy on the main couple that may have thrilling adventures but do so together. There are other ways to inject a romantic story line into a thriller or suspense title (see *Tell No One* below), but the majority of books hew closely to the romance pattern of throwing two people together who have a natural attraction and then using the thriller elements both to throw obstacles in the path to their happy ending and to give them something exciting to do besides just have sex. Where the variations in the blends usually show up are in the length of time it takes the central couple to get together and in the amount of suspenseful elements they must overcome. Some books (mostly highlighted in the romance chapter) spend a lot of time with the couple together, and the interactions between them (both sexual and not) get equal play with the thriller elements. Other blends focus more energy on the adrenaline plot—the serial killer, the missing person, the plot to kill the president—and sprinkle in the romance as more of a distraction. For some blends there might be a love interest, but she exists mainly to be rescued by the hero. These blends rarely have enough emotional weight to pull in fans of real romance. The romance in the blends I highlight here is certainly more than just a distraction, but the books have enough action and thrills to entertain those less interested in a love story. Even, perhaps, a fellow or two.

Tell No One by **Harlan Coben**

Although the most common way to combine adrenaline and romance is the female-centric romantic suspense genre, an example of a book that doesn't follow that formula but nonetheless has a strong romantic core that will appeal to both men and women is *Tell No One*. David Beck is a man haunted by the night his wife Elizabeth was brutally killed. Eight years later David is shocked out of his numb and grieving existence when he gets an e-mail that seems as if it could only have come from his dead wife. It might be a fake, but David won't stop until he finds Elizabeth, even if he must run from the police and a host of others who seem to want him dead before he finds out the truth. *Tell No One* has lots of standard thriller action, with a lone man on the run seeking truth and facing constant danger. But at its heart it is a deeply romantic story about a man who refuses to give up on the woman he loves. Most romances focus their energy on the woman's perspective and experience of love, but it is lovely to see the flipside of that. Readers do get some flashbacks to Elizabeth and David's initial love story; those will help deepen the emotional engagement with this couple so that we end up hoping just as much as David that somehow these two will be together again.

READING PATHS

If you like the suspense of a man haunted by a lost love and want a thriller:

Sleep No More by Greg Iles

If you like the grief-stricken protagonist and want romantic suspense:

Vanished by Karen Robards

The Witness by **Nora Roberts**

Women in peril are a standard trope in romantic suspense, usually involving a big strong man who saves the day. Nora Roberts flips this structure a little with a woman who is more than capable of saving herself. At 16, a sheltered but brilliant young girl witnessed a shooting involving a powerful Russian crime family. When the federal agents protecting her were betrayed and killed, that girl went on the run for years, landing eventually in a small artsy town in the Ozarks. Now going by the name Abigail Fowler, she's become an expert in computers and security, living quietly in a remote house at the end of town and trying to have as little contact as possible with the outside world. When Chief of Police Brooks Gleason sees Abigail, he finds her both an irresistible mystery and an alluring woman. The two circle each other, with the socially awkward Abigail baffled at the attentions of Brooks and attracted despite herself. The romance here is delicate and fragile, with Brooks coaxing Abigail out of her shell and making her realize she might want things she never thought she could have. Roberts also maintains the tension and suspense, never letting Abigail (or the reader) forget that there are still people who very much want her dead. But Abigail is strong, capable, unbelievably smart, and—eventually—determined to take back her life so she can build it with Brooks. Those Russians don't stand a chance.

READING PATHS

If you like the damaged and wary woman with computer skills and want an adrenaline read:

Monkeewrench by P. J. Tracy

If you like a woman on the run trying to reclaim her life and want more romance:

Pretend You Don't See Her by Mary Higgins Clark

Most Wanted by Michele Martinez (MELANIE VARGAS, BOOK 1)

Not every thriller that contains a romance is all about sex. Sometimes an author can do even more with smoldering attraction. When Federal Prosecutor Melanie Vargas catches a case involving a high-profile lawyer tortured and killed in his home, she thinks it is a career maker. But when witnesses start getting silenced and evidence gets stolen, it looks like there is a law-enforcement leak. Even though Melanie is going through a difficult separation from her husband and has a six-month-old baby, she really, really hopes the leak isn't charming FBI agent Dan O'Reilly. As a first novel (and the first book in a series), this is a strong thriller with the hope for future romance and should appeal to both adrenaline fans and romantics who just want Melanie to get a man who deserves her. So much of both thrillers and romance depends on having a lead character that you root for unreservedly, and strong, proud, Puerto Rican Melanie shows both her guts and her vulnerability to win over readers.

READING PATHS

If you like attorney/FBI action and want a suspenseful romance:

> *Sweet Talk* by Julie Garwood

If you like the strong female lawyer and want more of a thriller:

> *Final Jeopardy* by Linda Fairstein

Adrenaline/SF

The combination of adrenaline and science fiction is one of the more natural blends out there. Both genres have a high danger quotient and a love of technology. Techno-thrillers are a common way to blend some SF elements into a thriller. Secret labs, egomaniacal scientists, doctors who like to play god, and governments searching for world domination are all likely culprits to unleash something on the world that starts out looking like the future and ends up looking like a problem. Techno-thrillers are often a look at the dark side of technology. Whereas SF looks at where technology could take us and tends to see the wonder, thrillers often look at the dangers of technology outpacing ethical constraints. There are other interesting ways you can blend in SF to adrenaline besides near-future tech though. Because so much science fiction is fast-paced and mission-based, with exotic settings and military jargon, the fan crossover between adventure and military SF should be quite high. But once you leave planet earth, you are bound to leave some adrenaline fans behind. The key to finding SF blends that you can put into an adrenaline fan's hands is discovering something that focuses on the action and the human element of believable characters reacting to believable situations. Alien creatures and worlds might not be the first thing to try. Instead, keep it closer to home in terms of time periods and locales—readers will still have a taste of the wonders that could be explored.

Jurassic Park by Michael Crichton (JURASSIC PARK, BOOK 1)

There are lots of stories of scientists losing control of technology, but rarely has it been done in as spectacular fashion as with *Jurassic Park*. Billionaire John Hammond has brought paleontologists Alan Grant and Ellie Sattler to an island off Costa Rica to help him get his theme park ready to open. And what a theme! Hammond has worked with scientists to clone dinosaurs from ancient DNA and has created a kind of preserve for tourists to see the revived creatures. But there have been a few issues with the park, and it soon appears these are not small tweaks, but big miscalculations. Soon the dinos are loose, and all the technology put in place to control them proves to be useless. A large cast of characters is now in considerable danger, including Hammond's two grandchildren. A power failure ensures that they are isolated, and the dinos are even more dangerous than they had thought (watch out for the little ones—they spit). This classic combines the adrenaline aspects of thriller and adventure, but by spending time talking about the technology that went into the theme park and also the consequences of science outstripping ethics, SF and adrenaline fans alike should be pleased.

READING PATHS

If you like technology and ancient history and want more adventure:

Atlantis Found by Clive Cussler

If you like a story that explores cloning and want SF:

Kiln People by David Brin

The Revisionists by **Thomas Mullen**

Time traveling secret agents sounds like a pretty good setup for a quirky SF/thriller blend. At some point further along our time line an enormous disaster known as the "Great Conflagration" happens and paves the way for a perfect future—a future that includes time travel. Now there are people called "hags" traveling back to change things, and agents of the Department of Historical Integrity must travel back to stop them. Agent Zed must catch the hags and ensure that everything, good and bad, happens just as it should or his future won't come to be. He's been sent back to right before the Great Conflagration and insinuates himself into the lives of the contemps and the politics of the day, but this only makes his mission more difficult. A smart and complex thriller that plays with notions of fate and personal identity, the *Revisionists* starts rather slowly and seems fairly simple, but both the pace and the complexity of the narrative increase over the course of the book. It is fitting that there not be tidy endings for time travel stories, and this one will leave readers thinking after the last page is turned.

READING PATHS

If you like the time travel idea of people trying to change the past and want a thriller:

11/22/63 by Stephen King

If you like thought-provoking time travel and want more SF:

After the Fall, Before the Fall, During the Fall by Nancy Kress

---

Spiral by Paul McEuon

Where does science leave off and science fiction begin? This is a question at the heart of many adrenaline/SF blends. This thriller by a leading researcher in nanoscience starts with a flashback to young Liam Connor's work in WWII to stop the release by the Japanese of a deadly biological agent, and then jumps forward to an elderly Connor's apparent suicide. Both Connor's granddaughter and his research partner from the university where he taught are stunned, but they realize something is seriously wrong when an examination of Connor's body reveals that he had been tortured and that there were nanobots in his stomach. The race is on to find Connor's killer, who is planning to release a fungal biological weapon on the world, a fungus that would cause widespread hallucinations, violent outbursts, and death. They are aided by cryptic clues left behind by Connor himself, and the killer's motivations seem to go back to the darkest days of WWII. This near-future thriller has dangers that feel all too plausible, and the appealing characters and crisp dialogue keep readers turning pages. The author incorporates cutting-edge technology but also calls back to mostly forgotten history of biological weapons experiments in WWII to enhance this well-paced, well-plotted thriller. The technological and scientific ideas are presented in a very accessible way that will draw in even those not normally science-minded.

READING PATHS

If you like the biological weapon plot in WWII and want a thriller:

Ice Reich by William Dietrich

If you like the biological weaponry threat and want more SF:

Rainbows End by Vernor Vinge

WORKING WITH ADRENALINE BLENDS

How you approach adrenaline blends depends on whether you are starting from the point of view of a fan of the genre or someone who is more adrenaline resistant. For the fan, readers can find lots of choices here that will satisfy the itch for action, suspense, and adventure but still bring something new to adrenaline. For example, by adding in a new genre to temper the nonstop action of a thriller, readers can get an experience that has more depth than adrenaline alone. Adrenaline books can be the literary equivalent of a summer popcorn movie: best enjoyed if you don't think about the details too hard but just go along for the ride. The blending in of a historical frame or an SF idea or a fantasy element can add complexity and interest to the action or suspense. While there are plenty of fascinating plots in adrenaline, they can be somewhat tonally similar. Fans of adrenaline reads might turn to a blend when they want a new twist or a new background to the dangerous plots they are used to. Most of the blends here do not sacrifice any of the pacing traits that make up an adrenaline read; they simply add on to that pacing. On the other hand, there are readers who are not sure they want to read anything adrenaline based. They are afraid the action is too intense, the violence too graphic, and the plots too nerve racking. While blends in this chapter do tend to keep the action, there are lots of variation in levels of violence and scares. If a reader is truly afraid a book will make them lose sleep, the blends including adrenaline from the other chapters might be an easier sell. The extreme ratcheting up of tension that identifies an adrenaline read can be muffled a little by adding the frame or details of other genres, but readers have to want to be put on edge to enjoy even the blends. Any book that includes adrenaline is going to elevate the reader's pulse a bit, and that heightened experience is part of why readers keep coming back.

2

FANTASY BLENDS
Blends with Magic

Fantasy is a genre with many faces and blurry edges, which makes it hard to define. Rooted in our myths, fantasy can creep into virtually any work of fiction, sometimes seemingly without the author's conscious effort. To be considered a fantasy novel, the only thing required is that it take the reader to a different world containing magic and wonder. It doesn't have to be a completely new world in all its details and inhabitants. But something about the world and the things that happen there should tell readers that they are not in Kansas anymore. There used to be much more of a reliance on demonstrable, manifesting, capital-M Magic in fantasy: magical creatures, spells, wizards, enchanted objects, and so on. But fantasy is bigger than that, and there need not be a magical system if the world itself is different and transporting. The setting and trappings of a fantasy world are a big part of what defines it and what often draws readers to the genre. This frame can be a completely new world with different geography, customs, and laws of physics. Epic fantasy (also known as "second world" or "high fantasy") is usually rich in this kind of world building. But the fantasy world can be very similar to our own: city streets, regular people going about regular lives, but with an added layer of *otherness* that clearly marks it as a different version of our world. This branch of the genre is usually called urban fantasy, although skyscrapers are not required. Because the settings are by no means always urban, some prefer the label "low fantasy" to contrast with the imaginary worlds of "high fantasy" or "contemporary fantasy" as opposed to the history-influenced settings common in traditional fantasy. The two branches can attract the same fans, of course, due to their shared magical roots. But the different world-building techniques can also draw different readers. Even if frame is an appeal in both branches, they may each appeal to different audiences, as the frames are very different.

Epic fantasy and related subgenres often draw their frame from a medieval world, with castles, rigid social strata, and a low level of technology. It also usually has high stakes and world-threatening evil. The black-and-white morality that you find in the canonical traditional fantasies gets murkier with urban fantasy, and you are more likely to find your heroes making difficult compromises. But there are many writers bringing gritty antiheroes to traditional epic fantasy these days as well. Readers looking for a complete escape from reality are drawn to epic fantasy, which gives the reader the chance to vicariously experience things that could never happen to them. You will never be a young magician who would be heir to the throne if only you could defeat an orc army. That's ok. It can be thrilling and immersive to read about those things.

If the otherness of epic fantasy is a whole new world, urban fantasy's frame is often our world with all its problems but with the added wrinkle of magical creatures or abilities, sometimes hidden among us. The otherness in these books might be the ability to wield magic or the existence of vampires or our world's intersection with a fairy realm. A huge number of urban fantasies feature gritty real-world settings, crime investigations, and magical elements that exist hidden from the poor clueless norms. One of the most popular ways to tell this kind of our-world-but-not-our-world story is to have the setting be real in the broad strokes but altered in the particulars: a Pittsburgh half in and half out of Fairie (Wen Spencer's *Tinker*); an Atlanta where waves of magic sweep the streets in unpredictable tides (Ilona Andrew's Kate Daniels series); a Cincinnati where supernatural citizens are among us (Kim Harrison's Hollows series). The appeal of riffing on a real place is that it grounds readers, letting them know that this is a city street just like the one they know so well. Taking care of the mundane bits of the setting lets the writer spend more time on what makes their world fantastical. Although still an escape, most urban fantasy has a frame in which the readers *could* potentially picture themselves. Perhaps it is not likely that you will discover that your next-door neighbor is a werewolf, but if wrapped in the trappings of regular apartment-dwelling neighbor squabbles, it may not seem like such a leap.

APPEAL OF FANTASY

Like any genre, fantasy has many aspects and subgenres and, likewise, has lots of different appeals. The many branches of the fantasy tree all usually still call back to the same central appeal of a world where normal rules don't always apply and regular people can find themselves enmeshed in something magical, or maybe even find themselves becoming something magical themselves. The landscapes of fantasy are one of the biggest appeals of the genre. Fantasy fans love maps of the worlds they are reading about, but even without a map a fantasy world can transport readers. The imaginative lands readers visit might be completely, even surreally, different, or they might be familiar streets with a magical layer. Traveling to fantasy landscapes provides an escape from everyday life for readers, which can be one reason people are drawn to the genre. There is an emotional component to fantasy as well due to the battle of good versus evil that is common in many fantasies: the ordinary protagonist pitting himself against a powerful malevolent force. Fantasy relies on the reader emotionally engaging in this battle, sympathizing with the hero, and caring about the outcome. Because of its grounding in myths and fairy tales, the genre taps into our earliest stories, and that could be one of the appeals for readers. Those looking for a comfort read may find that the echoes of bedtime stories draw them to fantasy again and again. When working with patrons, there is another question you can ask to find out what they are looking for in a new read: do you want something close to real life, or as far from it as possible? Some people read for an experience in which they could see themselves walking in the protagonist's shoes. Urban fantasy is a good bet for that reading experience. Readers looking for that experience might be drawn to a protagonist of the same gender or to a setting in a familiar locale. Because fantasy elements can be sprinkled in lightly or draped over every aspect of the story, there is a wide range of books in the genre, making it easier to find one that appeals to any reader.

WHY BLEND?

Because fantasy is one of the genres that has a lot of classic elements and well-known tropes, it is one ripe for blending with other genres. A fantasy author's desire to play with expectations is one of the main reasons he will blend other genre elements, and there are a lot of expectations in fantasy fiction. Sometimes the blends are with genres that share characteristics. Being a genre with a high frame appeal, it crosses well with other frame genres, like historical fiction. Being an emotional genre, adding elements from another emotional genre like romance or horror leads to very natural blends. But you can cross with genres with vastly different appeal to good effect. A cross with an intellectual genre like mystery can bring a different audience to a book. Likewise, appeal characteristics that are more often found in other genres such as the pacing from an adrenaline genre book, can be blended into a fantasy to change its appeal. No matter what section of a library or bookstore a book is shelved in, it could also include a healthy dose of fantasy. This is because fantasy is one of the most popular genres to borrow from. Writers looking to inject whimsy or otherworldly elements into more traditional fiction reach into the fantasy genre bag of tricks.

THE BLENDS

Fantasy/Adrenaline

Fantasy is usually a fairly leisurely paced genre, spending time building and exploring invented landscapes. In particular, epic fantasy narratives are often very long with multivolume sagas quite common and individual books that can easily be used as a doorstop. It takes a while to settle into the story when there is a whole new world to describe. Even in the best fantasy, the authors are often so pleased with the magic system they have invented that readers must make their way through a lot of exposition before the plot even truly takes off. Then the plots themselves can be complicated: evil must be established and primed for toppling; protagonists must be plucked from the obscurity of a humdrum life to face their destiny; allies and boon companions must be collected and tools and skills obtained; and then there are often some trudging and traveling. Readers will probably get some action and danger, but the books are usually the kind that cause readers to wallow in the worlds created rather than jump right into events. This is changing somewhat, with modern fantasy writers more willing to plunge a reader right into their world and get to the plot. By blending in some elements from adrenaline, such as the action of an adventure story or the nail-biting suspense of a thriller, a fantasy writer can turn a languorous read into a page-turner. Epic fantasies are the most prone to the slowly unfolding narrative strung across multiple volumes and are less likely to be blended with adrenaline. Urban fantasy, on the other hand, has already picked up some tricks from adrenaline genres where the plot is often king and the world building can happen along the way. They are also more likely to have plot arcs contained in one (shorter) book, even if the book is part of a continuing series. The adrenaline plot of one man (or woman) up against overwhelming forces can also be a great blend with fantasy, as both genres share a love of the underdog.

The Lies of Locke Lamora by Scott Lynch (Gentleman Bastard, book 1)

Readers fond of crime capers featuring morally ambiguous characters with winning charm might have a new literary crush with Locke Lamora. He starts life, as so many good fantasy characters do, as an orphan. Rather than being destined for greatness in the epic fantasy mold (leading armies, wielding magic, etc.), Locke becomes the greatest con man in all of Camorr. Apprenticed to a rather select band of thieves who call themselves the Gentlemen Bastards, Locke and his friends spin their schemes to relieve the rich nobles of their accumulated wealth. When they get tangled up in a power struggle between rival criminal leaders, Locke (a rather soft-hearted criminal mastermind) finds himself just trying to keep himself and his friends alive. The characters of Locke and the Gentlemen Bastards are incredibly vivid, immensely likeable, and quite enjoyable to spend a few hours with. The author has an ear for dialogue, and his fantasy world is a gritty cityscape full of dark and dangerous alleyways. There is magic, and the system is a well-thought-out "word as power" variety, but Lynch wisely has the magic mostly offstage for much of the narrative. As the action escalates and various revenge schemes start intersecting, readers will race to find out Locke's fate. Those who like gritty fantasy, swashbuckling action adventure, and charming villains will enjoy this first book of an ongoing series.

READING PATHS

If you like the criminals in an imaginative cityscape and want a fantasy:

Among Thieves by Douglas Hulick

If you like the charismatic criminals and want a thriller:

The Hot Rock by Donald E. Westlake

The Rook by Daniel O'Malley

Myfanwy Thomas wakes up in a London park with no memory of who she is or why she is surrounded by dead bodies. Luckily there are two letters in her jacket, written by Myfanwy herself, telling her that she is a functionary in a supernatural spy agency called the Checquy Group and that she can either flee or try finding out who is trying to kill her. From this high-octane beginning, the story rockets around at an equally good clip. Myfanwy must essentially impersonate herself in her role as a Rook at Checquy, which protects Britain from supernatural threats. She learns that she was considered by her peers to be a glorified accountant, but without her memory she finds herself embracing a more forceful personality as well as a more active role, becoming a force to be reckoned with. The supernatural elements are fun, with monsters galore, evil plots to be foiled, and Myfanwy herself, who must learn to use her own special powers—underestimated until now. Author O'Malley has fun with the espionage thriller formula as well, employing a hefty dose of humor, but without compromising on the pulse-racing danger. The thriller trope of one man (or woman) alone and in deep waters while trying to ferret out a mole in his organization is turned up to an 11 here, with the addition of amnesia and supernatural bad guys both foreign and domestic. It's a wild, fun ride.

READING PATHS

If you like the secret organization dedicated to fighting supernatural threats and want fantasy:

B.P.R.D. (comic) by Mike Mignola

If you like the idea of a woman struggling with amnesia and want a thriller:

Before I Go to Sleep by S. J. Watson

Sandman Slim by Richard Kadrey
(SANDMAN SLIM, BOOK 1)

If a reader enjoys urban fantasy like Jim Butcher's *Dresden Files* but wants a darker, pulpier, faster read, this series featuring James Stark, aka Sandman Slim, might fill the bill. In book one, Stark is newly escaped from Hell. Yes, that Hell. He's back in Los Angeles after an 11-year stint "downtown," and he's gunning for those who sent him there. A mediocre magician before he went to Hell, Stark picked up a whole new bag of tricks as he fought for his life every day in gladiatorial cage matches for the amusement of a host of demons and fallen angels. Stark stalks his former magical associates through a noir L.A. cityscape where magic is hidden among the gaudy tourist traps and seedy city streets. Picking up allies and enemies along the way, Stark is focused and driven by revenge for both his entrapment in Hell and the death of the woman he loved. The violence quotient is quite high, and Stark is sarcastic, foul-mouthed, and bloody minded. Somehow, Kadrey finds the humanity in his antihero, and readers will root for Stark even when he is behaving quite badly (which is most of the time). Darkly funny, this series of books reads like urban fantasy with a horror chaser and an adrenaline kick in the pants.

READING PATHS

If you like the dark magician fighting against the odds and want a fantasy:

The Man with the Golden Torc by Simon R. Green

If you like the revenge plot and dark humor and want a thriller:

Skinny Dip by Carl Hiaasen

Fantasy/Historical

Because so many fantasy authors start their world building from the base camp of a real historical period, there is lots of overlap in appeal for these two genres. The degree to which the time period is recognizable as opposed to purely imaginative will help determine how to promote a book to a reader. The use of a known period as the basis for a novel's fantasy setting is a shortcut of sorts for an author. You may inject all sorts of magic and made-up details into a frame, but if you use the same words for small things like clothing, household items, and aristocratic titles you do not have to spend time defining your terms for the reader. Using details from history that the majority of readers are familiar with lets you jump more quickly into your story and obviates the need to do awkward info dumps via a character into whose dialogue you can stuff an explanation. Because both genres are what Joyce Saricks called "landscape" genres, they naturally appeal to readers who want a writer to spend some time filling in the details: the clothes, the transport, the smell of the streets. Readers of both genres want to be transported to another world. It is the degree to which a reader is open to that other world being more otherworldly that will help determine what book to put into their hands. A solidly fantasy book like George R. R. Martin's *A Game of Thrones* might appeal to an open-minded historical fiction fan because of the immense amount of detail put into the world. But even though the world has some of the trappings of a European medieval society, there are many differences and a magical element that might be a deal breaker for some readers. But non-magical historical fiction and fantasy blends also exist in which authors use a historical era for a pattern while changing enough details to make it clear it is not *our* history that they are telling, but a made-up world that mirrors our own. Whether a fantasy/historical fiction book has a little magic or a lot, as long as the story transports the reader to a world they want to explore, it will find an audience.

Across the Nightingale Floor by Lian Hearn (TALES OF THE OTORI, BOOK 1)

This first book of a series begins with a pseudo-historical setting based on medieval Japan and then layers in fantastical elements like warrior demons, magical ninjas, and supernatural powers. The hero of the story is Takeo, who has been raised among a secretive and peaceful people in the remote mountains of Japan. When an evil warlord destroys his village, he is rescued and adopted by the head of the Otori clan. Takeo soon discovers that he has special powers that mark him as a member of the Tribe by birthright, and he cannot help but wonder if Otori had reasons other than charity for taking him in. When his mentor is assassinated, Takeo will have a choice to make between two conflicting loyalties. The setting for this series will be catnip for those who enjoy tales of samurai and swordplay in medieval Japan but with plenty of fantastic and magical thrills. The whole series is a fascinating picture of a mystical never-was Japan, with politics and clan loyalties that combine with all the details of clothes and households to make you feel like you are there. But the fantasy elements are equally strong, not only with the action-packed plots full of supernatural battles, but in the bigger themes so common in good fantasy of destiny and fate.

READING PATHS

If you like the magically powered assassins and want a fantasy:

Assassin's Apprentice by Robin Hobb

If you like the Japanese setting and want historical fiction:

Shogun by James Clavell

His Majesty's Dragon by Naomi Novik (TEMERAIRE, BOOK 1)

If a reader ever wondered how different naval warfare would have been in the Napoleonic era if only they had dragons, this is the book that answers that question. *His Majesty's Dragon* is a delightful addition to the boy-and-his-dragon canon, mainly due to the fact that the boy is in fact a grown naval officer who never expected to be bonded to a dragon and the dragon is the magnificently drawn and nuanced Temeraire. Captain Will Laurence is a seasoned veteran of the ongoing conflict with Bonaparte's French navy when his ship captures a frigate carrying a priceless dragon egg. There is no time to get to port before the egg hatches, and Laurence becomes the hatchling's partner. Getting Temeraire for the British Navy is quite a coup, for dragons make up an important part of the combatants in this alternate-history of the Napoleonic Wars. It is, however, quite an adjustment for Laurence, who must leave the regular navy and join the understaffed and underappreciated Aerial Corps. The story is stuffed with enough thrilling aerial battles and tactical discussions to satisfy any historical adventure junkie, but the real trick is how Novik seamlessly weaves dragons into this military world. Fantasy fans need not fear an overload of jargon, though, as the heart of the story is still the relationship between Laurence and Temeraire.

READING PATHS

If you like the dragon-and-human relationship and want fantasy:

Eragon by Christopher Paolini

If you like the naval adventure and want straight historical fiction:

Master and Commander by Patrick O'Brian

Jonathan Strange & Mr. Norrell by Susanna Clarke

This is one of the truly mystifying success stories in fantasy publishing. Not because the book is not deserving of every bit of the attention and best-seller status that it achieved, but because there doesn't seem to be a particularly easy explanation for why a book about rival magicians in 19th-century England would capture the wide readership that it did. The book is long, chock full of weird and wonderful footnotes (providing information both historical and magical), and not particularly fast-paced. But it is also fascinatingly detailed in its world building: both the early 19th-century world we know from history books and the secret world of magic practitioners. Despite all its challenges, *Jonathan Strange & Mr. Norrell* is a book that readers sink into and wallow around in. The characters are lovingly drawn and exceedingly complex, as is their milieu: a world where magic is on the brink of extinction. Gilbert Norrell is the last known practitioner of magic until Jonathan Strange enters the scene. Norrell takes the young talent on as an apprentice, but his desire to control Strange leads inevitably to conflict. Strange wants to bring magic back into the world by way of the mysterious Raven King, a powerful magician from England's past who dwells now in Faerie. The narrative weaves in and out of the Faerie realms and Regency ballrooms, and seems equally comfortable in both. It's an amazing achievement sure to thrill those who like challenging fantasy novels as well as those interested in the Napoleonic era.

READING PATHS

If you like the Regency-era setting and want a fantasy:

Glamour in Glass by Mary Robinette Kowal

If you like the Regency-era setting and want historical fiction:

An Infamous Army by Georgette Heyer

Fantasy/Horror

The horror genre has gone through a lot of changes in recent decades. While once hugely popular, some of its dedicated publishers have gone under in recent years, and some of the core authors have moved on to other genres. One of the ways that horror has found a sneaky new niche is to hunker down in the dark back corners of the fantasy genre. Dark fantasy is a genre that could exist solely to market to those fans that loved early creepy books by Stephen King, Clive Barker, and Peter Straub. When it became no longer popular to market something with scary supernatural elements as horror, the obvious next-door neighbor to borrow a label from is fantasy. While you could always find a lot of cheerful young protagonists off on a quest in fantasy, there has also always been a dark current running under the genre. Even the light and tune-filled Disney versions of fairy tales can trace their roots to the sinister stories collected by Charles Perrault and the Brothers Grimm. Like horror, fantasy is very concerned with Evil with a capital E. Dark bargains, monstrous creatures, and life-threatening danger can be found in both genres. And when the vampires and werewolves in literature needed a genre to hang out in when horror started disappearing, they flocked to fantasy. The difference between horror vampires (to use them as an example) and fantasy vampires is that while they are still the monsters that were invented by the horror genre, in fantasy they are more likely to be nuanced and complex monsters, even allies or lovers. This is a big difference, as the monster in horror must usually remain mostly unknowable and "other" in order to stalk and scare human prey (and readers) more effectively. The biggest way that writers blend horror and fantasy these days is that they borrow the atmosphere and tone from horror to give their fantasy novels that feeling of darkness, dread, and creeping chills readers used to find in books from the horror aisle.

The Drowning Girl by Caitlín R. Kiernan

What is real and what is imagined can blur for anyone, but adding mental illness to the mix adds a level of the surreal to the narrative by one of dark fantasy and horror's most respected authors. India Morgan Phelps (Imp) knows that she is most likely crazy because she comes from a long line of crazy women. This makes her the ultimate unreliable narrator, as she writes and rewrites her own memoir in an effort to exorcise the images that plague her waking and dreaming mind. Imp's schizophrenia seems under control until she meets Eva Canning, a woman who looks just like the subject of a painting she is obsessed with called *The Drowning Girl*. She transfers her obsession to Eva, trying to find out everything about her, but her own memories and perceptions cannot be trusted. Dreamy in the way it weaves poetry and prose, Imp's spiraling sense of her own insanity nevertheless gives this work a suspenseful urgency. When Eva disappears, Imp tries to piece together what she knows and what she only imagines to fill in the story. Mermaids and werewolves and ghosts create echoes of fairy tales, but in Kiernan's hands they are darker than any bedtime story.

READING PATHS

If you like the unreliable narrator and not knowing what is and is not real and want fantasy:

Legion by Brandon Sanderson

If you like the unreliable narrator and not knowing what is and is not real and want horror:

The Tale of Raw Head and Bloody Bones by Jack Wolf

Perdido Street Station by China Miéville (NEW CROBUZON, BOOK 1)

In this genre-defying work, Miéville uses language that twists and dives in stunning, showy arabesques to create a vivid cityscape called New Crobuzon. The city has many inhabitants from dozens of species, all living side by side in its close and mostly squalor-filled confines. Outsider scientist Isaac is working on a new unified theory when he is asked to help Yagharek, a garuda who has had his wings removed but who desperately wants to find a way to fly again. Isaac's research into all things flying unwittingly leads to a threat being loosed on the city—slake-moths that can eat the dreams and consciousness of any sentient victim. The plot unfolds slowly at first, as Miéville delights in Dickensian levels of description, but eventually enthralls, especially as the chase to find and eliminate the threat of the moths takes over the plot. The amazing fantasy world filled with exotic peoples would be appealing on its own, but there is also added genre interest from the steampunk details of calculation engines, dirigibles, and robotic constructs. The other genre element that runs underneath the story is a strong thread of horror, which comes into the story first from the extreme close-up that Miéville focuses on the grotesqueries of his non-human city dwellers. Then there are the slake-moths, truly scary horror monsters that can mesmerize you with one look at their hypnotic wings and then take from you everything that matters. The way that Miéville intricately weaves his genres and his story lines together is amazingly, dizzyingly inventive.

READING PATHS

If you like the dark world, intricate plotting, and description and want a fantasy:

Titus Groan by Mervyn Peake

If you like the monster loose in the city and want more horror:

Monster by Frank Peretti

Something Wicked This Way Comes by Ray Bradbury

This iconic novel by the versatile Bradbury shows that sometimes a book doesn't so much blend genres, but teeters in between them. Two 13-year-old protagonists embody this idea, with Will Halloway being born one minute before midnight on Halloween and Jim Nightshade being born one minute after midnight. The two are inseparable in the way that only childhood friends can be, running around their midwestern town with a freedom of a bygone age. When a mysterious carnival comes to town, it appears to be the stuff of dreams, and Jim and Will sneak out in the middle of the night to watch it set up. At first it seems wonderful—the smell of cotton candy and the music of the calliope an irresistible lure. But when the boys meet the proprietors of Cooger and Dark's Pandemonium Shadow Show and see their dark carousel, they realize the whole town is in grave danger. Although this slim narrative has a fairy-tale-like power, the real strength of the book is in the amazing imagery and atmosphere. As is often the case with powerful examples of both fantasy and horror, the narrative is a very simple story of good versus evil and the power of love and laughter over darker emotions and intentions. But what is amazing is the way that Bradbury captures the wonder and dangers of the edges of childhood. This is the ultimate seasonal book, made for long midwestern October evenings when summer is a fond memory and winter a chill foreboding.

READING PATHS

If you like the carnival, where magic is real and dangerous, and want a fantasy:

The Night Circus by Erin Morgenstern

If you like the dark look at the power of childhood fears and want horror:

The Tooth Fairy by Graham Joyce

Fantasy/Mystery

Blending mystery into any genre is often an attempt to give the story a different structure. Whereas in most mainstream fantasy the plot arcs follow certain well-traveled paths (coming-of-age story, hero's quest, etc.), adding a mystery gives writers different hooks on which to hang a plot. For example, a common mystery arc is as follows: a crime is committed; someone is brought in to investigate; clues are discovered; crime is solved; guilty parties are punished. By adding these elements to a fantasy, you have this plot progression moving your narrative along, which can give you an entirely different appeal. While there are always various impediments to the investigation in a mystery, in a fantasy blend those impediments might just turn out to be magical creatures intent on world domination. The stakes get raised with the fantasy at the forefront, as fantasy often deals with people trying to save the world. Although fantasy/ mystery blends can be done beautifully in an epic fantasy setting, they are more often found in the mirror worlds created for urban fantasy. Because urban fantasy relies on a starting point of our own world and all its problems, it makes sense that crime would appear in its plots. Most (but not all) urban fantasies include some kind of investigatory puzzle, although the emphasis they place on the puzzle determines whether they can be considered true fantasy/mystery blends. Why fantasy and crime seem to go together so well might be the real mystery. They are just as likely to have kick-ass female heroines as broody rough-guy heroes, which could be one reason for their popularity among both genders.

Rosemary and Rue by Seanan McGuire (OCTOBER DAYE, BOOK 1)

In this opening book of a series about halfling Fae October "Toby" Daye, she is newly freed from a spell that kept her trapped in the form of a fish for 14 years. A pretty difficult adjustment is made even harder when someone from Toby's past is murdered and while dying lays a curse on Toby that compels her to find the killer. Toby wants nothing more than to hide in the mundane world and try not to think about what she lost, but the case promises to draw her back into the dangerous waters of Fae politics. This series gets better and better over time, but the first volume shows all the promise of an author with a deft hand at creating a heroine who is strong but vulnerable and who always tries to do the right thing. Her world where the faerie folk live hidden among us is one full of vicious dangers and wistful beauty. As Toby moves from the back alleys of San Francisco to the halls of the lords of the Summerlands, every creature we meet is more interesting than the last. The Fae are scary and alluring and, as a creature half-Fae and half-human, Toby straddles both worlds in an uneasy balance. The mystery of who killed Evening Winterrose is a great puzzle, and Toby's need to find the killer before the curse kills her adds urgency to a fast-moving plot.

READING PATHS

If you like the plot that involves navigating Faery politics and want a fantasy:

War for the Oaks by Emma Bull

If you like the San Francisco setting and strong heroine and want a mystery:

A Grave Talent by Laurie R. King

The Eyre Affair by Jasper Fforde (THURSDAY NEXT, BOOK 1)

If you've ever loved a book so much you wish you could inhabit it, *The Eyre Affair* could be read as a cautionary tale. In the inventive universe created by Fforde, an evil arch villain named Acheron Hades has opened portals that allow people to cross over into works of literature, and he has sent one of his henchmen to kill a minor character in a Dickens book, thereby forever changing the story. Fforde's world is an alternate Great Britain circa 1985 where the Crimean War is still going on, dodos have been brought back from extinction, and literature has a completely central role in people's lives. Children swap literary trading cards, Shakespeare is an audience participation event à la *Rocky Horror Picture Show*, and there is a detective force dedicated to protecting the written word. Thursday Next is one of those literary detectives, and her uncle created the Prose Portal that is being used by Hades to hold characters from beloved works of fiction for ransom. When Hades' Dickensian caper is foiled, he steals the manuscript for *Jane Eyre*, and Thursday pursues the villain into Bronte's novel to save Jane . . . and *Jane*. Action-packed and extremely quirky, this is less a whodunit than a crime caper–style mystery. The villain is known, but the pitting of criminal versus detective is a satisfying one for fans of mysteries, who will also like the fact that this volume kicks off a whole series of literary (really) mysteries.

READING PATHS

If you like the literature-based magical world and want a fantasy:

The City of Dreaming Books by Walter Moers

If you like the literary-world focus but want a straightforward mystery:

Booked to Die by John Dunning

Finch by Jeff VanderMeer

In Ambergris, human inhabitants labor for the ruling gray caps, a sentient fungal race that took over the once-famous city after civil wars left a power vacuum. The fungi let Ambergris fall into a state of moldy decay and don't particularly care about humans, although they use them as cheap labor and, in the case of John Finch, as lowly police detectives. Finch tries to toe the line in the department, which is difficult when his mushroom boss speaks in nothing but squeaks and clicks. His world is completely shaken, however, when he catches a case that appears to involve the double homicide of a human and a gray cap. VanderMeer drops readers immediately into the action of the investigation, and he doesn't spend a lot of time explaining the vividly weird world as he builds it around the reader. The noir trappings are plentiful: femme fatales, criminal underworlds, betrayals, and a dogged detective with a secret past. But the way the action unfolds is a little choppy, the language sometimes abrupt and sometimes baroque, and the bizarreness of the world so acute that the reader is left slightly off balance. This seems intentional and both suits the noir aspects of the story and adds to the surreal enjoyment of this invented world. Finch is determined in his pursuit of the truth, and those open to a unique reading experience will enjoy following him down the rabbit hole of Ambergris's gritty streets.

READING PATHS

If you like the surreal cityscape and want more fantasy:

The Etched City by K. J. Bishop

If you like the detective forced to work for an oppressive regime and want a mystery:

A Corpse in the Koryo by James Church

Fantasy/Romance

Some of the biggest names in fantasy these days are women, and while having a female author doesn't guarantee that a book will have a romance, it does seem that women authors in all genres are more open to adding a love story to their fiction than men. There are men just as capable of writing a moving romantic arc, but they just seem less likely to make it the focus of a story. This boom in female fantasy authorship (and readership) means that those who like a little romance with their magic have no shortage of choices. Romance can be added effectively to a variety of fantasy stories, and while some blended categories took some hunting to find a set of great examples, with this pairing it merely took a short spin through the stacks to find some favorites. While I discussed urban fantasy under the fantasy/mystery blend, there is another subgenre of books that is closely related but more focused on relationships. This subgenre, paranormal romance, is one usually marketed squarely at the romance readers, but some books with that label could easily be handed to an urban fantasy fan. Many of the long-running series in the urban fantasy genre often incorporate a love interest for the protagonist eventually, although the romance might not last more than a book or two. Fantasy heroes and heroines have pretty complicated and difficult lives, so why should their love lives be any different? The series aspect that is so important in fantasy genre does mean that a romance over more than one book is probably going to have some ups and downs in order to remain a driving part in the plot. The key to finding the right blend for fantasy fans is to know what they are looking for in terms of the amount of romance and sexual content. A brief mention of the fact that the book has a fair amount of "sexy bits" is usually enough to know whether a reader is open to paranormal romance or whether it might be better to steer them back to more traditional fantasy. Adding romance to fantasy stories is a great way to make characters more sympathetic and make the costs of their quest or struggle more immediate. A romantic relationship can be a great complication in a plot, creating conflict for a hero or heroine who must choose between personal happiness and a greater goal. Romance can also emphasize the humanity of any supernatural characters. The longing for happily ever after is common to fictional characters and readers alike, making this a blend that can be satisfying.

Poison Study by Maria V. Snyder (STUDY, BOOK 1)

Yelena is awaiting execution in the dungeons of the Commander of Ixia when she is given an unexpected reprieve to become the palace's new food taster. Learning to detect the slightest presence of poison is a small challenge compared to navigating the difficult political waters of the court. Her guide to both is Valek, the Commander's chief of security, a mysterious figure who has complete control over Yelena's fate. As she slowly discovers she not only has a role to play in Ixia's future but also has powers she never dreamed of, Yelena must stay ahead of the people who want her dead. This is an intriguing variation on the typical medieval fantasy world, organized along military lines and with magic completely outlawed. When Yelena meets a magician from another land, she realizes that she will have to decide where her loyalties lie: with those who might train her to use her hidden powers or with Valek who has earned her trust and perhaps much more. The slow burn of Valek and Yelena's relationship moves from a very unequal footing where Valek holds all the power over Yelena's very life to a place of mutual appreciation and eventually attraction. This is not a bed-hopping romance by any means (despite the come-hither look of the cover), but it is a very appealing romantic story line in a strong fantasy narrative.

READING PATHS

If you like the story of a woman reprieved from death and sold into service and want a fantasy:

> *Throne of Glass* by Sarah J. Maas

If you like the story of a woman who starts as a prisoner and want a romance:

> *Surrender* by Pamela Clare

Beguilement by Lois McMaster Bujold (THE SHARING KNIFE, BOOK 1)

This series of fantasy novels follows the adventures and building relationship of Fawn, a young farmer girl, and Dag, a seasoned patroller from the Lakewalker people. Fawn is pregnant at the beginning of the first book, *Beguilement*, and desperate to get away from her farm community and leave behind the gossip of her neighbors and quarrels with her family. She soon runs into mortal peril when she encounters a "malice," an evil creature able to take human form, and only survives through the help of Lakewalker patrolman Dag. In the struggles against the creature, Fawn has lost her child, and somehow the baby's spirit imbues Dag's sharing knife. Dag must report this development to his people, and he convinces Fawn to accompany him to Lakewalker headquarters. Along the way, Dag and Fawn fall in love, but their backgrounds and life experiences are very different. The romance is very sweet and works mainly because of the well-drawn characters of Fawn and Dag. The age difference between the two might make some readers wince, but Bujold does a good job of showing how the two actually complement each other well. The fantasy world and its magic and perils are not hugely detailed in this first volume but will be explored further as the series goes on.

READING PATHS

If you like the young farm girl off to find adventure and want a fantasy:

Arrows of the Queen by Mercedes Lackey

If you like the lovers of different ages and backgrounds being meant for each other and want a romance:

Kiss of Snow by Nalini Singh

Cry Wolf by Patricia Briggs (ALPHA AND OMEGA, BOOK 1)

Many urban fantasy series feature romances, but they often build slowly over multiple books. If readers would like a series that doesn't stint on the world building (it's set in the same world as Briggs's other series featuring Mercedes Thompson) but that also has a love story at its heart, they should give *Cry Wolf* a try. Anna is a rare Omega wolf, outside of the pack order and able to calm and control other wolves. She had been horribly abused by her former pack but was rescued by Charles, the son of the leader of all the Packs. Charles is an Alpha wolf, used by his father, the Marrok, as the enforcer of the Pack laws. The two are mated at the beginning of this story, which means that their wolves at least are sure they belong together. Anna must learn what being an Omega means, and she and Charles must both find a way to fit into each other's lives. This novel has a lot of classic romance elements that turn out to also be great fantasy tropes such as a soul mate relationship and a woman who appears weak and helpless but who discovers she has a power of her own. The relationship and trust build throughout in a very satisfying way and, although the book is more fantasy-plot heavy in the second half as the couple go after a rogue werewolf, we get to keep exploring how Charles and Anna both want each other and need each other. Fantasy fans, especially of Briggs's other werewolf series, will enjoy the deeper look we get at the Marrok's pack and werewolf politics and powers.

READING PATHS

If you like the werewolves but want a fantasy:

The Wolf Gift by Anne Rice

If you like the couple that are bound together but who must also find a way to live together and want a romance:

Mating Instinct by Katie Reus

Fantasy/Science Fiction

Although magic and science are sometimes placed at opposite ends of the speculative fiction spectrum, they do not have to be completely incompatible. The intrinsic nature that science fiction and fantasy share as literatures of the imagination means they are really genres that live side by side. The thing that separates the genres is possibility. Science fiction posits worlds filled with wonder and weirdness, but it is all possible—not today maybe, but possible. Fantasy similarly imagines other worlds, but the worlds created are no longer bound to the rules that they have to be possible or even probable. They might be worlds that we *wish* could be true (or in dark fantasy *fear* instead), but science and logic tell us they are not possible. So how do you blend the two? An author can of course simply say that magic and science coexist and write his fictional world accordingly. There is also a subgenre of SF called the planetary romance where the action takes place on another world, usually exotic in its look, feel, and culture. These worlds can seem very like fantasy worlds in their powerful landscapes. The most common way to blend SF and fantasy is to build worlds that the reader thinks are impossible but then reveal that they only *seemed* impossible; it might have looked like magic, but really it was science all along. This is not an easy juggling trick. Once you have built a satisfying world that seems made of magic, why would you want to bring it back to reality? But when done well, this can be a way for authors to have their cake and eat it too. Readers get the unlimited imagination that a fantasy world can encourage, but the author can make it rational as well. The advantage to this kind of ingenious blending is that both fan bases can take away what they want from a book.

Black Sun Rising by C. S. Friedman (COLDFIRE TRILOGY, BOOK 1)

The origin of the planet of Erna as a lost colony of earth is established early in this first volume of a trilogy and is referred to throughout the narrative. But despite the reminder that this is SF, the world of Erna is awash in magical powers that humans try to both harness and wield. One of the great SF themes of the book is the human race's proclivity for tinkering with the land and flora and fauna surrounding us to better mold things into a perceived ideal. This turns out to be especially dangerous on Erna. The original colonists encountered a land that was their last best hope for a new outpost for humanity and settled there despite the presence of a native power that was seemingly linked to the tectonic activity of the planet. The *fae* is a force imbuing every aspect of the planet with a power that can be used by certain adepts to give themselves magic-like abilities. Some, such as the healer-priest Damien, use the abilities for good. Others, such as the centuries-old adept known as the Hunter, harness dark *fae* forces to drain other creatures of the life force. Damien and the Hunter must work together to help Ciani, a female adept who has been robbed of her memories by a *fae*-wielder so powerful that the whole world is in danger. The world Friedman created here is an amazing work of science fantasy, with a believably scientific grounding and a thoroughly magic-filled story.

READING PATHS

If you like the good vs. evil struggle and want a fantasy:

Tigana by Guy Gavriel Kay

If you like the setting of a world where wild powers can be harnessed to human will and want SF:

Dune by Frank Herbert

Dragonflight by Anne McCaffrey (DRAGONRIDERS OF PERN, BOOK 1)

The Pern books are another great example of SF that reads like fantasy. There are many things about the Pern books that scream "Fantasy!" to readers, such as a young girl with a big destiny, a feudal society, telepathic communication, and of course, dragons. But McCaffrey always held that they were SF, and there are things that back her up: the dragons are genetically engineered, and there is no magic beyond the telepathic bond that riders have with their dragons. At the beginning of *Dragonflight*, Lessa, the last surviving legitimate heir to Ruatha Hold, will do anything to get back what is hers. Disguising herself as a servant, Lessa decides to use the arrival at Ruatha of one of the famed dragonriders to try to overthrow the usurper who killed her family and rules at Ruatha. But Dragonrider F'lar is traveling the Holds to find candidates for a new clutch of dragon eggs and recognizes that Lessa's ferocious strength of will and mental talents might be just what is needed to bond with the rare and precious queen dragon when she is born. Lessa must choose between her revenge and the chance at a whole new world as a dragonrider. What only the dragonriders remember is that danger threatens the planet and only the dragons can save Pern. The world building of Pern and its society are enthralling for both SF and fantasy fans, with details about the look and feel and smell of the places all adding up to a world that is fully realized in this first book but that will provide imaginative soil for dozens more.

READING PATHS

If you love the dragons and human interaction and want fantasy:

Dragonsbane by Barbara Hambly

If you like the planetary romance with its vivid world building and characters with big destinies and want SF:

Jaran by Kate Elliott

The Shadow of the Torturer by Gene Wolfe
(BOOK OF THE NEW SUN, BOOK 1)

An intriguing way to mix a medieval-ish fantasy world with futuristic storytelling is to go so far into the future that civilization has collapsed back to something that looks like the past. We meet Severian as an apprentice with the guild of Torturers, a despised and feared but traditional part of society under the reign of the Autarch. The first half of the book is spent in the decaying halls of the Citadel, but when Severian falls in love with a prisoner he is meant to torture and allows her to die, he is exiled. Action picks up remarkably as Severian sets out for his new assignment in a remote district. While trying to buy a garment to cover the distinctive cloak of his order, he meets up with some con men, gets challenged to a duel, is involved in a carriage race (and crash), and much more. A dizzying amount of information is thrown at the reader in this first book in a series (including fun Easter eggs spelling out the links between our world and Severian's for the reader paying attention), and some of it will come in handy later. Some of it is simply the rambling that gives verisimilitude to a narrative that is supposed to be an old man looking back on a long life. Dense with archaic language and philosophical and religious allusions, the books in this series are no easy read. But the power of Wolfe's vision is worth the effort. Imagining what the Earth (here called Urth) might be like when civilization is so old that the sun is dying is a great creative setup that will be explored further in the rest of the Book of the New Sun series.

READING PATHS

If you like the dense prose and imaginative far-future worlds and want a fantasy:

> *Lord of Light* by Roger Zelazny

If you like the world of a decaying post-tech future and want SF:

> *The Dying Earth* by Jack Vance

WORKING WITH FANTASY BLENDS

Some genres, once introduced to a book, take over completely so that it is hard for them to be read as anything but that genre. Fantasy isn't like that. You can find fantasy in small doses where a character or situation just seems a little otherworldly, all the way to huge world-spanning invented landscapes with elaborate magic systems and wondrous creatures on every page. The range of magic and weirdness in the fantasy recipes means that it's quite easy to find a blend that will work with a reader. The key question to ask in a readers' advisory situation is whether or not readers want something familiar so they can imagine the events of a book happening to them. Fantasy, when present in a big way, tends to dominate the other genres in a blend. In the other chapters I give examples of books where the fantasy is measured in smaller doses, allowing the other genre a chance to shine. But even with the fantasy-forward blends here, there is still a range of fantasy elements, from whimsical to completely otherworldly. Are the readers open to visiting a new world with magic and monsters? Then a blend based on the epic end of fantasy could work. If they prefer a setting closer to reality and the magic to be subtler, a blend that starts from an urban fantasy base might work better. Being open to at least a little weirdness is probably the only requirement to handing someone a blend that includes fantasy. But be careful, as one taste of magic can be enough to hook susceptible readers into a serious fantasy habit.

3

HISTORICAL FICTION BLENDS
Blends from the Past

Historical fiction is the genre for lovers of the past. It's a feast for the senses, giving readers the sights, sounds, and even smells of the historical setting it employs. Setting is part of the appeal characteristics that can be grouped under the heading "Frame." The frame of a story is more than simply its physical setting. Although the time and place in which a book is set are part of it, there are also elements of atmosphere and tone. Frame is a big draw for many readers, and two books with the same geographical and time setting can manifest very different frames, depending on those other elements. A historical fiction novel has a distinct frame that by definition includes a setting in the past. However, whether historical fiction is a genre or not is open for debate. The question exists because the *only* thing that defines historical fiction is that the setting is a time period in the past, often further narrowed to a time period prior to the lifetime of the author (Saricks 2009). In one sense this means that historical fiction is a great mixer, as adding a historical setting to another genre instantly results in a blend. But there are some further characteristics of classic historical fiction, the most important of which is that the book is not merely set in a specific time and place but seems to transport the reader there. Some historical fiction is very focused, revolving around a particular time or significant event and showing how characters lived in that time or reacted to that event. There are also examples of historical fiction that have a more sweeping focus on a person or group of people and follow them through a period of time, showing how the passage of time and events affects the characters. Historical fiction can take place in any time in the past and any place, although there are some subgenres that are specific to their settings, such as westerns.

Writers of historical fiction have a special challenge. Not that any sort of creative writing is easy, but while general fiction authors need to create characters and put them into situations, the frame they work in is one that they might live in (or could at least visit), making sure they get all the details correct. Science fiction and fantasy writers also have to construct a frame, but they get to use their imagination to fill in the broad strokes and the details. The challenge of historical fiction is that to be effective a writer needs to get it *right*. The setting is the past; usually a very particular time and place. And that means research because if the author gets the facts wrong or fails to achieve an authentic experience for the reader, the book will not resonate. Whether the novel is set 3,000 years in the past or just a few generations before the present, the challenge for the writer of historical fiction is to immerse the reader in that time and place. The most effective historical fiction feels as if it could not possibly be set in any other time or place. The setting is not just incidental to the story but is often just as important as any character to how the story unfolds. Unlike some of the other genres in fiction, in which there is a formula or pattern that readers expect and writers write to, historical fiction does not follow any particular narrative beats. Instead its only rule is to make the frame come alive.

There are examples of books with historical settings in every other genre, so are they historical fiction? Or is historical fiction simply any book with a setting in the past that doesn't happen to fall into another genre? And if not, what identifies historical fiction novels as a recognizable, promotable genre? For the purposes of this book, I define historical fiction as any book in which the historical frame is completely integral to the story.

APPEAL OF HISTORICAL FICTION

In her book on genre fiction, Saricks has placed historical fiction alongside fantasy as a landscape genre. The reason that these two genres (along with westerns) go together is that they share a focus on creating a detailed background for their stories whereby the look and feel of the world are as important as many other elements in the book. If you've ever read a book and felt like the setting was almost another character in the story, then you have found a writer with a great skill at creating frame. Historical fiction needs to take you somewhere. If genre fiction is derided by some as escapist reading, I would like to go on record as saying that an escape into literature is not something to be denigrated. If a book can take you somewhere else with your imagination and if, as in the best reading experiences, you also take something back with you, those are surely journeys worth taking. In historical fiction what readers take away, if the writers have done their work well, is a greater knowledge of a piece of history and a perspective on the human experience of that time and place. The best historical fiction is as carefully researched as any work of nonfiction history and packed with facts. Where the alchemy takes place is that those facts and the research behind them are woven together so seamlessly with the story that the reader absorbs them without even realizing it. Many readers find historical fiction an approachable way to read about history, as it gives them a point-of-view character through which to witness that history. Any good historian can present facts, but the narrative where you get to vicariously *live* through history with a character is a different experience. The dusty history we struggled to learn in school can suddenly come alive in a great historical fiction novel, providing an enjoyable way to swallow facts that were indigestible when presented in a textbook. Readers get not just the big picture of a time period, but also a sense of how an individual would have experienced that time. Learning was never so fun as in historical fiction.

WHY BLEND?

Unlike genres where you can point to characteristics of plot to determine the nature of a novel, historical fiction is defined by its frame and especially its setting. A blend with literary or general fiction is typically what people think of when they label a book historical fiction—stories of people and relationships in a historical setting, without any other genre characteristics. A reason for writers of historical fiction to blend in genre is because they want a particular set of narrative trappings. Although the setting can move a novel along and put characters into motion if it is a time of upheaval or great change (as is common in historical fiction), sometimes a plot needs a little something extra. While for fans of the genre a simple story of people living their lives against the backdrop of history is enough, for others the addition of a mystery, a love story, or a bit of suspense can add dimension and interest to a novel.

THE BLENDS

Historical Fiction/Adrenaline

Most historical fiction is set in exciting times. Simply choosing a time period of conflict and change can inject adrenaline into a story. Surviving times of change and upheaval can put characters into adventure mode, which is why historical adventure is a popular subgenre. But that is not the only way to blend in adrenaline. There are great examples of historical thrillers that blend an interesting setting and a fast-paced, suspenseful story line. Spy thrillers are a popular way to use this kind of blending. WWII through the Cold War years was a golden age of espionage and is an attractive setting for writers who like the straightforwardness of good guys versus bad guys, which can be projected much more easily on the political enemies of our past than on those of our present. But any time period can be the setting for a thriller if a writer can paint a vivid enough picture, not only of the setting, but also of the dangers and obstacles faced by the protagonist. The essence of many a good thriller is a lone man up against impossible odds, and that can happen in any time. Adding the historical frame simply opens up more options for the writer to make his characters' survival more chancy. When a character is in a jam *and* has no access to the Internet or a cell phone to get out of that jam, an author needs to get creative. All of this has the potential to make the narrative even more suspenseful and enjoyable for the reader than the same story in our own time period.

Napoleon's Pyramids by William Dietrich (ETHAN GAGE, BOOK 1)

American Ethan Gage is having a fun time cavorting around revolutionary-era Paris when he wins a mysterious medallion in a card game. This sets in motion all the rollicking adventures that follow as Gage joins up with Napoleon's army to avoid being framed for murder by someone who also wants the trinket. As a part of the scientific cohort accompanying the army, he takes part in the French invasion of Egypt and begins to realize his medallion is tied to secrets of ancient Egypt. The action is nonstop from the streets of Paris to the beaches of Alexandria and the alleys of Cairo and finally to the Great Pyramids of Giza. Napoleon is interested in power wherever he can find it, which means that between the indomitable Corsican, murderous Arabs, and a heretical French Freemason, Ethan has collected a lot of people who want what he has or want him dead. Luckily, he is a likeable fish out of water who finds allies (and even love) in his search for knowledge. The pacing will satisfy those who like action-packed thrillers, but Dietrich also revels in puzzles both mathematical and human and has a deep appreciation for his historical setting. If he has a slight tendency to overstuff the plot with the important events of the time (Ethan runs into Lord Nelson and takes part in the Battle of the Nile), Dietrich never fails to make readers feel like they are there in the thick of things.

READING PATHS

If you like the Napoleonic wartime setting but want more historical fiction:

Sharpe's Rifles by Bernard Cornwell

If you like the investigation of ancient mysteries and want a thriller:

The Last Templar by Raymond Khoury

Captain Alatriste by Arturo Perez-Reverte (ALATRISTE, BOOK 1)

In a shout out to the adventure tales of old, Spanish author Arturo Perez-Reverte has a whole series of books set in 16th-century Spain featuring swordsman-for-hire and sometime-assassin Diego Alatriste. In this first volume, Alatriste is hired by a pair of hooded men to accost a couple of Englishmen and recover anything they were carrying. As they engage, he is impressed by the fighting spirit of his targets and begins to believe that he has been misled in his assignment. By sparing the foreigners, Alatriste has pitted himself against some powerful and dangerous people, including a rival assassin and the forces of the infamous Inquisition. Reminiscent of an Errol Flynn movie in its swashing and buckling, the lone man of honor (if not necessarily goodness) up against forces of corruption and power is a great trope from the thriller arena. The pace is swift, and the short length makes this book feel even more like an adventure serial of the past. Alatriste's young ward and squire Inigo Balboa lives with the man and acts as the book's narrator, which allows us to view a larger-than-life character through the eyes of a character in his shadow but also closely placed to assist the swordsman at crucial moments. The portrayal of a glorious empire on the decline is filled with lovely details of the gritty streets of Madrid as well as the corridors of power. Perez-Reverte has a deft hand at dialogue, and even in translation this helps transport readers to his historical setting. Alatriste is a product of his time, living through war and upheaval and struggling to maintain the personal code that means everything to him.

READING PATHS

If you like the setting in Golden Age Spain and want historical fiction:

The Queen's Vow by C. W. Gortner

If you like the pacing and action of an assassin's tale but want more adrenaline:

Rain Fall by Barry Eisler

Mission to Paris by Alan Furst

Spy novels are mainstays of the adrenaline genres, and they can range from the cerebral cat-and-mouse tales of suspense for which John Le Carré is justly famous to action-packed, globetrotting, car-chasing extravaganzas. Alan Furst tends to fall in the middle of that continuum. He writes brainy puzzles with a dose of action. One problem with the quickly changing political and technological landscape is that spying has changed over the years as well. That leads writers who like to tell stories of human intelligence officers running around the capitals of Europe to use a historical setting. Furst has an oeuvre of novels set in WWII-era Europe, and this recent volume is another winner. Employing the glamorous backdrop of moviemaking, in *Mission to Paris* Furst brings the reader to France in the last year before the German invasion. Frederic Stahl is a Hollywood actor whose studio loaned him out to make a movie in Paris, but it didn't know that Stahl is harboring secrets. Because he grew up in Austria, Stahl is targeted by German intelligence and propaganda operatives to push forward their pro-Nazi agenda, but the actor has a mind of his own. There are dozens of suspenseful close calls and tense moments as Furst paints another perfect portrait of WWII-era Europe.

READING PATHS

If you like the setting of WWII-era Europe and want more historical fiction:

A Thread of Grace by Mary Doria Russell

If you like the espionage and want more adrenaline:

Spycatcher by Matthew Dunn

Historical Fiction/Fantasy

Many fantasy settings are based closely on real historical periods. The degree to which the author goes on to add details and flights of fancy to that familiar period varies from novel to novel and helps determine whether a book will appeal more to fans of one genre or the other. The use of real history as the frame for a fantasy novel shifts some of the world-building focus from what the world looks like to the author's more imaginative elements. In other words, a castle is a castle, so let's not waste time describing why certain people live in castles and get right to the magic bits. But because both historical fiction and fantasy focus a lot of energy on description and creating vivid worlds, writers of blends must still flesh out the sights and smells of the worlds they create. There are lots of ways that an author can incorporate history into a fantasy. Magic portals to the past can be fun, as can fantasy worlds that resemble our own history but change the place names and facts to leave more room to play. Authors can stay very close to the historical record, but imagine how things would be different if there were magic in the world. These types of books are really a form of alternate history, a subgenre that often appears under the category of science fiction (if it doesn't have magic). Because so many pre-Christian societies believed in gods and spirits that could act in the world, the inclusion of magic in a story of ancient history can seem like a natural part of the world that the characters inhabit. I've chosen blends here to appeal to historical fiction fans, so they all share a deep respect for historical research. If there is one thing that will tick off a fan of historical fiction, it is getting the history *wrong*. Having a little fun with a time period is allowed, but whatever else authors do, they need to still be true to the period details that historical fiction readers love.

Under Heaven by Guy Gavriel Kay (Under Heaven, book 1)

> Here is an example of an author who has a penchant for taking a known historical period as his template and then tweaking it enough so it's difficult to tell whether the book will appeal more to fans of historical fiction or fantasy. This book and its sequel are set in ancient China. Well . . . not exactly. The place names are different and the year is never explicitly stated, but the details of speech, dress, government, and lifestyle are all drawn meticulously from chronicles of China's Tang dynasty. The reason that I have kept it in this chapter is because the fantastical elements that Kay employs are subtle and read more like the fanciful touches found in contemporary poetry of the period. As *Under Heaven* opens, Shen Tai is nearing the end of a herculean

task burying the slain soldiers from a battle in remote Kitai, his only company the ghosts of the dead. As a reward for his honorable service to both the dead of his own country and those of Kitai's enemies, he is given a gift of 250 horses. This is wealth unimaginable for the soldier and makes him a target for many powerful and ruthless forces. The journey of Shen Tai through the country to the Imperial seat is the kind of great quest adventure found in epic fantasy, but it is easy to forget that this is a work of imaginative literature when the details all seem so right. Whether readers experience it as a never-told, never-been history of ancient China or a work of realistic fantasy, the pages of this enormous book almost turn themselves.

READING PATHS

If you like the setting of Ancient China but want more historical fiction:

A Floating Life by Simon Elegant

If you like a pseudo-historical setting and a hero trying to navigate the political sphere in fantasy:

Range of Ghosts by Elizabeth Bear

The Mists of Avalon by Marion Zimmer Bradley (AVALON, BOOK 1)

Choosing a period of history shrouded in myth leaves an author plenty of room for embellishments both mundane and fantastical. The story of Arthur and his court has been told and retold in every generation and is replete with magic and enchantment but far fewer facts, which leaves room for a new take on the story. Bradley breathes fresh life into the old tale by giving readers a new female perspective on the power struggles and tragedies that have previously been focused on the King and his unfaithful wife. Arthur's half-sister Morgaine (known in many versions as Morgan le Fey) is a pagan priestess of Avalon and the main focus of Bradley's story, which pits her and her aunt Viviane, as worshippers of the old Druidic gods, against those who wish Britain will convert to Christianity. These early Christians include Gwenhwyfar, Arthur's new bride, and Lancelet, a knight with ties to Avalon but whose destiny is tangled with Gwenhwyfar and Arthur. The pace is slow and filled with myriad details of how women (and men) lived, fought, and worshipped in ancient Britain. Having the women's perspective on the power struggles of the time, as well as showing how the women had a species of power themselves, gives this old story new life. The fantasy comes in with the mystical nature of Avalon and the power granted to the priestesses of the old gods. This book will transport readers into the myth and make it seem very real—an experience that will appeal to fans of both genres.

READING PATHS

If you like the politics and struggles behind the myth of King Arthur but want more historical fiction:

The Winter King by Bernard Cornwell

If you like the mix of Arthurian legend and magic and want more fantasy elements:

Taliesin by Stephen R. Lawhead

Territory by Emma Bull

One great way to root a historically set novel in a specific time and place is to include real historical figures as characters. The protagonist, of course, can be a well-known person from history, but it is easier (and more fun) to tell a story that people think they know from a point of view they do not expect. Bull has taken the classic Old West story of the gunfight at the O.K. Corral and imbued it with magic and freshness by shifting focus. Rather than telling her story from one of the more famous residents of Tombstone such as Wyatt Earp or Doc Holliday, she introduces us to Mildred Benjamin. Mildred is a widow living quietly in the frontier town before the arrival of horse trainer Jesse Fox. Jesse has been drawn to the territory by his teacher, a Chinese wielder of magic named Chow Lung. He soon learns that there are other powerful sorcerers in Tombstone and that they do not care whom they hurt if it gains them what they want. With Mildred's help, Jesse squares off against the chilly menace of a magically talented Wyatt Earp, putting a great new spin on a classic story. By introducing the magical elements slowly, Bull allows her historical setting to flourish. The baking heat of the Arizona sun, the mud in the streets after the sudden rains, and the frequent and casual violence all transport readers to the American frontier. Emma Bull is one of fantasy's most talented writers, known for creating vivid and compelling characters. Readers will respond not only to the proper widow Mildred, torn between propriety and adventure, but also to Bull's fresh take on the Earps and the charismatic drunken gambler Doc Holliday.

READING PATHS

If you like the new perspective on the Old West and want historical fiction:

Doc by Mary Doria Russell

If you like the Old West setting but want fantasy:

A Book of Tongues by Gemma Files

Historical Fiction/Horror

Historical fiction is a genre known for its research and scholarship, all put to use in the service of fantastic storytelling. Adding a supernatural genre like horror to the mix is not done often, but that doesn't mean it can't be a great blend. Terrifying stories can happen in any time or place. The added challenge that a writer takes on by removing the story from a setting familiar to their readers is that it adds a little distance. And distance is not always conducive to a good scare. Most horror counts on giving readers a vicarious thrill, making their hair rise and their skin creep as they imagine what it would be like if the scary thing happening were happening to them. While this is by no means impossible with a book set in the past, it is certainly easier if it is set in a time and place readers are familiar with. But fans of historical fiction are already open to taking that imaginative leap of picturing a story in a setting that is unfamiliar. That is *why* they like historical fiction. Although historical fiction can often be disturbing or even frightening (wartime, primitive medicine, and archaic personal hygiene are just a few things that can cause a reader to shudder), readers approaching a historical/horror blend should be prepared for something darker, scarier, and more violent than anything usually found in historical fiction. Adding a creepy or scary story to a well-built historical setting is a great way to add tension, plot, and obstacles as the characters try to get to the bottom of the nature of the horror at play.

The Terror by Dan Simmons

An ill-fated expedition to find the Northwest Passage ends in blood and, well, terror. Sir John Franklin was a real explorer who disappeared in 1845 after setting sail from England to find a sea route through the Arctic Ocean by way of Northern Canada. Simmons's novel imagines what might have happened to the expedition. The main protagonist is the captain of one of Franklin's ships, Francis Crozier, who considers Franklin a blowhard and a fool, but readers also get different perspectives on the ill-fated voyage from several other participants on this voyage to uncharted territory. The terror comes into play not only in the very real horrors that the crew suffered on this voyage that they all soon came to believe was nothing but a death sentence—frostbite, disease, accidents, starvation, and more—but also from a mysterious supernatural *something* that appears from nowhere across the ice and kills the crew in spectacularly bloody fashion. The punch of frenzied action that these attacks bring to the story are a welcome bit of punctuation in what would be the fascinating but slow demise of the crew. Gruesome in its portrayal of the conditions the ice-bound explorers endured, the details of the undertaking are meticulously researched and will make curious readers immediately want to learn more about the Franklin Expedition. As creepily scary as the arctic monster is in the story, the actions that the sailors took against each other as conditions worsened are just as horrifying.

READING PATHS

If you like the detailed look at another expedition (this one to find Franklin's lost crew) but want straight historical fiction:

The Voyage of the Narwhal by Andrea Barrett

If you like the Arctic setting and the menace from the ice and want horror:

Who Goes There? (novella) by John W. Campbell Jr.

Commedia della Morte by Chelsea Quinn Yarbro

For those who like the *idea* of horror more than many of the trappings of that genre, Chelsea Quinn Yarbro's series of books featuring vampire Count Saint-Germain is an ideal choice. He's a vampire, a creature that could be considered a founding father of the horror genre, but he's pretty subtle about it. The women he chooses to slake his blood thirst are usually quite willing, although repeat donations can lead to them joining his vampiric ranks. But because of the near-immortal nature of vampires in Yarbro's take, readers get a chance through the many, many books of the series to visit any historical setting the author desires: Ancient Egypt, Rome, Russia, and more all get volumes in the series, and all are meticulously researched. In this 25th entry, Saint-Germain is called upon to rescue an old lover (and fellow vampire) from the clutches of the tribunals of the French Revolution. Madelaine (who also appears in the very first book in the series, *Hotel Transylvania*) is living a life of luxury in France when the revolution and its zealous prosecution of the wealthy sets its sights on her. She writes to Saint-Germain, who sneaks into France in the company of an acting troupe and sets about trying to get to Madelaine before she is executed as a traitor. The setting is described in loving detail, both through the eyes of the characters and through dispatches from the tribunals, which gives a chilling portrait of the period known rightly as the Terror. For those who prefer their vampires urbane and seductive, Saint-Germain will be a character they will love to follow through the ages.

READING PATHS

If you like the look at the excesses of the French Revolution and want historical fiction:

Madame Tussaud by Michelle Moran

If you like the suave version of vampire as seducer but want more of the kick of horror:

Interview with the Vampire by Anne Rice

Those Across the River by Christopher Buehlman

Haunted by terrible memories of WWI and more recent scandals that lost him his university position, Frank Nichols has moved to the small town of Whitbrow, Georgia, where he has inherited a house from a long-lost relative. Accompanied by his girlfriend Dora (the cause of his scandalous dismissal), the couple pose as husband and wife while Frank sets about researching his family in hopes of writing a book. The insular and creepy townspeople have a strange custom of sending pigs across the river at the edge of town each year, but Frank and Dora help cast the votes to discontinue the tradition. The problem is that if those living on the other side of the river don't get their tribute of pigs to eat they're going to come looking for something else to satisfy their appetites. The picture of Depression-era life in a Southern small town is crafted with care and does not stint in painting the details of poverty, racism, and vigilante justice. When the horror kicks in and the monstrous neighbors come to town, there is a shocking change of tone. But the writing is so very fine, even in its shocking violence, that this book will appeal to fans beyond the horror genre.

READING PATHS

If you like the Jim Crow–era South setting and the dark past casting a shadow over a town but want historical fiction:

Cane River by Lalita Tademy

If you like the dark secret of a small town and want horror:

Salem's Lot by Stephen King

Historical Fiction/Mystery

Because most historical mysteries have a great deal of respect for their setting, the titles from the mystery chapter that are historical fiction blends are often equally appealing to the historical fiction fan. But whereas in those books the setting is detailed and fascinating, it is not quite as embedded in the story as it is in the books that I have chosen for this chapter. Here we have fascinating frames being built, and yet they are still in service to a satisfying mystery. With mysteries, the focus is often very much on plot (crime, investigation, and resolution) as well as on characters. The puzzles of who did it and why are big reasons why people pick up mysteries, regardless of when they are set. The formula of mysteries is comforting, but this doesn't mean a reader doesn't like to change things up every now and again. The need for a break from a beloved genre might mean quitting mysteries entirely, but a less drastic way to reenergize a mystery reader is to give her something with that added interest of a unique and compelling historical setting. The bonus to setting a mystery in the past is that you almost always automatically add a level of difficulty for a book's detective. The tools that modern detectives have at their disposal—fingerprinting, computers, and good grief, cell phones!—all help to catch criminals. If the crime solvers in a mystery don't have those tools, they must be much more creative than if they did. Although you can set any mystery in the past, the books here could not take place in any other time than the one their author chose. The setting is wound tightly with the plot so that one does not work without the other. One of the most appealing aspects of reading historical fiction is that it points out that human beings haven't changed much over the millennia—and at no time is that more evident than when reading about the crimes we commit upon each other.

A Conspiracy of Paper by **David Liss** (Benjamin Weaver, book 1)

It's not that easy being a Jewish ex-prizefighter in 18th-century London, and Benjamin Weaver struggles mightily to carve out a life for himself as an enforcer of debts, a taker of thieves, and a perpetual outsider. When his estranged father dies under suspicious circumstances, Benjamin is drawn into an investigation that leads him to the Byzantine inner workings of the nascent stock-trading world and the bitter rivalry between the Bank of England and the South Sea Company. It's an unlikely setting to provide such drama, but Liss does a great job of making the world of these traders understandable even to those who don't know how today's stock market works. He obviously did an incredible amount of research, and the end result is a detailed and believable world. As he shows us his London, we get to know Weaver, a character who belongs nowhere so he can go anywhere. He is a tough but savvy bruiser and an ideal guide to the world both highbrow and low, and as he searches for his father's killer, this twisty mystery will keep you guessing.

READING PATHS

If you like the background of seedy 18th-century London and want historical fiction:

Slammerkin by Emma Donoghue

If you like the intertwining of history and finance and want a mystery:

The Death Instinct by Jed Rubenfeld

The Name of the Rose by **Umberto Eco**

When several monks are murdered in a 14th-century Italian abbey, visiting investigator Brother William of Baskerville sets aside his initial task of rooting out possible heretics to apply his considerable logical and deductive abilities to solving the crime. With the help of his assistant (and our narrator), the novice monk Adso, Baskerville finds a convoluted mystery involving a rare Aristotelian manuscript, poison ink, and a crazy blind monk. This is a long book with lots of diversions and discourses, but the patient reader will be rewarded with a gripping climax, with all loose ends tied. Baskerville and Adso operate as a kind of medieval Holmes and Watson, with a cunning adversary they must work to uncover. On the historical front, we get not only a vivid picture of monastic life of the age, but also the papal and royal politics of that time. All the names and sects and, egads, Latin seem daunting at first, but the narrative is strong enough to pull the reader through. Not really a traditional mystery or what people usually expect in a historical fiction work, *The Name of the Rose* nevertheless manages to be a very cool play on both genres while also being a highly erudite and philosophical work of literary fiction.

READING PATHS

If you like the medieval setting and rising conflict of church and state and want historical fiction:

World Without End by Ken Follett

If you like the setting of a monastic order and want a mystery:

The Beautiful Mystery by Louise Penny

Mistress of the Art of Death by Ariana Franklin

Adelia Aguilar is a graduate of Salerno's School of Medicine, summoned to Cambridge, England, by none other than the king, Henry II. Adelia is an expert at discovering causes of death, but in 12th-century England her skills could get her branded as a witch. The case Henry has her looking into is a political and religious hot potato—four children have been brutally murdered in Cambridge, and blame lands on the local Jews. With the help of a cast of fascinating characters such as her Moorish servant Mansur and local tax collector (and inappropriate love interest) Rowley Picot, Adelia tries to get to the bottom of the deaths. The character of a female doctor in the 12th century could seem like a hopelessly anachronistic attempt to have a spunky modern heroine, but the backstory of her upbringing and education are well-researched and convincing, and Adelia herself is complex and appealing. The details of the time, from domestic scenes to royal politics, all paint a vivid picture with no wasted set decoration. The mystery showcases the darkest impulses of humanity, and although Adelia doesn't lack for suspects, she uses every tool at her disposal to get justice for the murdered children and to prevent an unjust persecution of the Jews of England. This is the first of a marvelous series that was sadly cut short by the 2011 death of the author, who also wrote historical romances under her real name, Diana Norman.

READING PATHS

If you like the detailed portrait of 12th-century England and want historical fiction:

> *When Christ and His Saints Slept* by Sharon Kay Penman

If you like the complex mystery with strong women ahead of their time and want a mystery:

> *Poison* by Sara Poole

Historical Fiction/Romance

There is a huge (and hugely popular) subgenre in romance devoted to romances in historical settings. Some of these historical romances merely use their settings in history as a fun excuse to talk about pretty clothes or fancy balls. Even when they are meticulously researched (and many are), their marketing and the tight focus on the romance make these a less than automatic suggestion for historical fiction fans. For this chapter, my goal was to look for those historical fiction novels that have a compelling and satisfying love story at their center. These are not hard to find, as the pursuit of romantic love is one of the prime plot motivators in many a book regardless of genre. This plot could happen in any novel: boy and girl meet but conflict separates them. It's what happens *around* that plot that makes it a genre book. To be considered even a blended romance, the couple should be affected by the historical period but not overshadowed by it. In a historical fiction/romance blend the historical setting is usually the source of the conflict that keeps the hero and heroine apart. History is actually *great* at creating reasons people can't be together! What makes a book work for fans of both genres is that it has a great grasp of a historical time period so the reader understands what's keeping them apart *and* cares deeply enough for the two lovebirds to want desperately for them to end up together. That is also a deciding factor in why I excluded some very romantic titles. If the story is swooningly romantic but the couple is kept apart in the end, it will not satisfy most romance fans, who tend to be addicted to the happily-ever-after ending.

The Winter Rose by Jennifer Donnelly (Tea Rose Trilogy, book 2)

> Donnelly has penned a series of fat novels set around the turn of the last century that are stuffed to the brim with historical color. In this middle volume, India Selwyn Jones comes from money but turns her

back on her family in order to pursue a medical career in the poorest slums of London. The biggest tie left to her old life is her engagement to childhood friend Freddie Lytton, a ruthlessly ambitious politician who will do anything to keep India and her dowry. Everything changes when an injured Sid Malone is brought into India's hospital. Sid is a criminal—head of a massive ring of thieves, prostitutes, and drug dealers—but he didn't start out like that. In fact, his real name is Charlie Finnegan, and he is the brother of tea mogul Fiona, the heroine of Donnelly's first book, *The Tea Rose*. Attraction flares between Sid and India, and improbably enough they fall in love. This is a book for fans of big romantic historical fiction, such as that of Barbara Taylor Bradford, and has plenty of details that paint a picture of the time, including medical treatment in the late 19th century and political upheaval as the new Labour party comes onto the scene. We also get an armchair traveler's view of London society, high and low, and even an excursion to British East Africa. The love story might be a bit unlikely, but Donnelly is a dab hand at creating characters that readers will bond with, who will keep them turning the pages.

READING PATHS

If you like the setting amid the slums of London and want more historical fiction:

The Crimson Petal and the White by Michel Faber

If you like the love story between a woman from the upper classes and a man of the slums and want a romance:

A Lady Never Surrenders by Sabrina Jeffries

Katherine by Anya Seton

Royal romances in history rarely end well, considering all the dynastic politics, marriages of convenience, and general obstacles history throws at the powerful. One of the most famous romantic love stories in England's medieval past is between John of Gaunt, middle son of King Edward III, and Katherine Swynford. When they meet in Seton's well-researched novel, Katherine has come to court a beautiful but penniless girl of 15 and is almost immediately betrothed to a rough Saxon knight, Hugh Swynford. Her marriage is not particularly happy, and when she falls into the orbit of the dashing and newly widowed John they begin an affair that will last for the rest of their lives. Seton gives ample background for readers unfamiliar with the 14th-century Plantagenet-ruled England but never lets her research bog down the story. The details of medieval Europe are richly described, including things like the clothes and food and trappings of daily life. But the relationships between the characters are what truly bring this story to life. Despite the many difficulties faced by the central couple, not the least of which is the fact that John was wed to another for most of their years together, they get that rare thing in historical fiction based on real history: a happy ending. When John is finally free, the two wed, and their newly legitimized children became the progenitors of the royal line that sits on the throne of England to this day.

READING PATHS

If you like the period around the Hundred Years' War and want more historical fiction:

The Archer's Tale by Bernard Cornwell

If you like the medieval setting and want more of a romance:

By Arrangement by Madeline Hunter

Outlander by Diana Gabaldon (OUTLANDER, BOOK 1)

Starting from a very fantastical premise of a woman magically traveling back in time to the 18th century (bonus fantasy genre!), this romantic novel soon settles into very satisfying historical fiction. Claire Randall is on her second honeymoon in the Scottish Highlands in 1945 when she takes a walk amid an ancient stone circle only to suddenly find herself in the year 1743. Upon arrival, she is assaulted by a British soldier and rescued by a band of Scottish raiders who take her in and give her shelter. Claire adapts well to her precarious situation within the clan, but her biggest conflict comes from the passion she comes to feel for one of her rescuers, Jamie Fraser. She must decide whether to make a life with him in the past or to try to find a way back to her own time. Having fish-out-of-water Claire tell this story is a very clever way to allow for an exploration of the detail of this tumultuous period of Scottish history that would seem like awkward exposition if done by a character more embedded in the time. The details of life in the Highlands paint a vivid picture, but it is the thrilling story full of swashbuckling action and high romance that will pull a reader in. Watching two strong characters bend to each other and overcome huge obstacles to be with each other will be satisfying for romance fans who like their love stories with an epic sweep. The fact that Claire is a woman out of her own time adds poignancy to her choice to love the Highlander. This is the first book in an ongoing series featuring Claire and Jamie and the tumultuous times they lived through.

READING PATHS

If you like the background of the Jacobite uprisings and want historical fiction:

White Rose Rebel by Janet Paisley

If you like the fish-out-of-water heroine and a Scottish setting and want a romance:

The Wedding by Julie Garwood

Historical Fiction/SF

The combination of historical fiction (a genre focused on exploring the past) and science fiction (a genre focused on the future) is not one that you come across very often in the stacks. Historical fiction is a genre that tries to be true to the facts, whereas science fiction may start from facts, but then it is all about extrapolating from those facts into the imaginary (albeit possible) future. Although both genres are about world building to a certain degree, their aims seem diametrically opposed. Historical fiction wants to take the reader to an era that is not their own. It wants readers to feel as if they are walking the streets and experiencing the events of a bygone age. Science fiction often looks at where we are going instead of where we have been. In a very real sense, however, they both are about projecting our present-day consciousness into another time. If SF explicitly wonders "what if?" and spends its energies on thinking about how humans would deal with the obstacles and events of a future world, historical fiction does the same thing in reverse. Historical novels are influenced by the time about which they were written, and inevitably the author is trying to get readers to think about why people did things the way they did in the past, what we've learned from them, and how we (the modern reader) would react to that time. Blending the two is difficult but not impossible. One way to create a satisfying blend is through a time-travel narrative. If the time-travel mechanism is technological rather than magical, it is considered SF. We get a point-of-view character from our own time who experiences an authentic trip to the past. Alternate histories can also be considered historical fiction/SF blends as they start from a "what if?" place and spend their time exploring history. Steampunk is a truly interesting genre that has blossomed in recent years, using all the fabulous details such as the costumes and furnishings of the past, which are the bread and butter of historical fiction, but imagining that history taking a strange new turn. It is alternative history but with a very particular sensibility that looks pointedly to the Victorian era and wonders what would happen if technology stayed steam powered. Such a weird idea to have inspired dozens of novels, influenced TV and movies, and spawned a whole subculture! Although there are steampunk works that are squarely SF, they tend to read more like historical fiction because of the loving attention paid to the trappings of the past. No matter how an author puts the two genres together, the resulting blend has the unique task of showing us a picture of the past but giving it an imaginative, speculative twist that can appeal to readers of both historical fiction and science fiction.

Yellow Blue Tibia by **Adam Roberts**

Although this novel is arguably set in too recent a period of history to be counted as historical fiction, it does such a marvelous job of painting a picture of the time that I could not resist including it. The novel begins in the 1940s in a remote dacha in Russia. Five science fiction authors are brought there to meet with Stalin, who sets them to the task of writing a narrative of an alien invasion, as he believes there will be a post-war need to unite the people against a common enemy to better control them. They leave after completing the story, not really thinking about it again. Forty years later one of these writers, Konstantin Skvorecky, is tracked down by his old collaborator who now works for the government and believes that the story they wrote is coming true. The paranoia and oppression of the last days of the Soviet era are brought to life vividly, as is the character of Konstantin—cranky, burnt-out, and yet gamely amused by almost every crazy turn of events. The plot veers from farce to tense action and back again. Historical fiction fans will appreciate the picture Roberts paints of a culture tipped on the knife's edge of change. At the same time, UFO conspiracists could find a lot to love, depending on whether you squint through Konstantin's ironic eyes or choose to believe. It's a quirky book that could find a broad audience, no matter what genre is preferred.

READING PATHS

If you like the humor and details of life in Soviet Russia and want historical fiction:

> *City of Thieves* by David Benioff

If you like alien invasion stories with a historical background that read like science fiction:

> *Worldwar: In the Balance* by Harry Turtledove

The Astounding, the Amazing, and the Unknown by Paul Malmont

Loosely arranged around the true fact that several SF writers from the golden age of pulps worked together in a lab for the US Navy during WWII, Malmont has stretched that fact into a historical adventure story that John W. Campbell would have been happy to have run in his magazines. With icons of science fiction like Robert Heinlein, Isaac Asimov, and L. Sprague de Camp as characters, the appeal for the SF fan should be fairly obvious. The young men are all working together at a navy lab in 1943 Philadelphia trying to turn their enormous imaginations into real inventions to aid the war effort when they stumble upon some old research of Nikola Tesla. With the aid of a motley array of other writers (including a vivid portrait of a young L. Ron Hubbard) the group attempts to figure out the mysteries of one of Tesla's greatest and most dangerous lost inventions: a tower that might be the key to unlimited free energy for the world. The pace is breakneck, as befits a paean to the pulps, but does linger long enough with our characters to get a glimpse of the personal dramas that drove these soon-to-be-famous writers. Malmont puts his theme into the mouth of none other than Albert Einstein, who when helping out Heinlein and Asimov, says that science inspired science fiction but science fiction also serves to inspire and spur science to even greater achievements. The fun of this work is not only its pulpy action, but also the great portrait of a period when the US government was willing to try some crazy stuff to stay ahead of the Nazis in scientific achievement.

READING PATHS

If you like the glimpse of the pulp era but want historical fiction:

> *The Amazing Adventures of Kavalier and Clay* by Michael Chabon

If you like the WWII setting and a dose of intrigue and want more science fiction:

Cryptonomicon by Neal Stephenson

The Difference Engine by William Gibson and Bruce Sterling

In this steampunk team-up of two of SF's biggest names, we get an alternate version of 1855 London when the Industrial Revolution kicks off early due to the invention by Charles Babbage of steam-powered cybernetic Engines (computers!) 100 years sooner than in our own history. The fascinating SF "what if?" of the novel is to explore what huge changes would have been wrought on a Victorian society suddenly plunged into the Information Age. There is a fun but slightly shaggy and convoluted plot involving various characters vying for possession of a special set of punched cards for an Engine. We get enough historical details of dress, geography, and society of the time to recognize them and see how they have been changed. The technobabble will appeal most to those with a grounding in Babbage and early efforts at mechanical computing, but the real science fictional accomplishment is the reenvisioning of the world under the new paradigm of an early computer age. As one of the first steampunk books to reach a large audience (it was nominated for a Nebula in 1991), this novel succeeds in showing how you can wed the wonder of science fiction to the nostalgia of historical fiction and end up with something entirely new.

READING PATHS

If you liked early mathematicians Ada Lovelace and Charles Babbage and want historical fiction:

Lord Byron's Novel by John Crowley

If you like the computer crime but want thoroughly modern science fiction:

Halting State by Charles Stross

WORKING WITH HISTORICAL FICTION BLENDS

If you find patrons who like historical fiction, they are probably at least a little open to any good story that will transport them to a vividly realized time and place. Because the characteristics and appeal of historical fiction are not plot based, this potentially leaves all your genre options open. If there is a genre that a reader has always been curious about, mixing it with historical fiction might be a way to find him a gateway into that genre. Find out what draws him to historical fiction. Is it a particular time period? It is usually possible to find a blend that scratches that itch. But some readers don't care about the particular setting as long as they can have that you-are-there experience. Some genres seem to go together with historical fiction like peanut butter goes with jelly, and they have correspondingly huge presences in the marketplace. Historical romances and historical mysteries are just two examples. Even if the genre does not scream for a historical setting, there are still new and interesting stories to tell when you take that genre and send it to the past. Every book has the capacity to take readers someplace new and teach them something they didn't know, but if you blend in a great historical frame, you might enjoy the added travel through time.

4

HORROR BLENDS
Blends That Give You Goosebumps

Horror is the genre that taps into our darkest fears. In these books, the heroes or heroines are usually threatened by some unexplainable menace that leaves them (and the reader) feeling helpless and afraid. The menace is often supernatural, but need not always be, as long as the atmosphere and emotions of fear and dread are evoked. Horror is mostly known for its monsters, such as ghosts, vampires, werewolves, satanic manifestations, and all sorts of other creatures that go bump in the night. But what really defines horror is humanity's struggles over forces of darkness. Oh, and it should scare the pants off you. The horror genre is in a bit of a state of flux these days. From its heyday in the 1980s when Stephen King was reliably putting out a horror book each year and there were mainstream publishers dedicating big chunks of their list to the genre, we have seen a decline on the print side. Even at its height of popularity, a lot of the publishers of horror were small and independent, and the tougher economic climate for publishing has meant that dozens of them have gone under. One of the largest, Leisure Books, went under in recent years, eliminating one of the most reliable outlets for print horror. In addition, some of the bigger stars of horror have started moving away from the genre, at least in the way their books are marketed. Publishers that might have once published a book as horror now seem much more likely to call it something else such as "supernatural thriller" or "dark fantasy." This vacuum and remarketing didn't kill print horror though. Small presses (always an important part of the horror landscape) like Bad Moon, ChiZine, Cemetery Dance, and others have quietly taken up the slack and continue to publish books that are proud to have "HORROR" stamped on their covers.

The market may have shrunk, but the genre still has many fans. In a way, horror is stronger than ever in media as a whole: hit TV shows like

The Walking Dead, movies like *Cabin in the Woods*, and video games like *Left 4 Dead* show that the public's appetite for gore and scares remains strong. And these newer works often play with the genre in smart ways as well, using the tropes and trappings as ways to tell stories that are often ironic or self-referential. New horror works, both in print and media, also seem very interested in taking what works best in horror—creeping dread, inescapable evil, shocking gore, and spine-tingling scares—and mixing in elements from other genres. In this way, horror has benefited hugely from the trend of genre blending, finding a way into books like primordial ooze sneaking through narrative cracks and filling the voids where the author needs to inspire a good scare.

APPEAL OF HORROR

Horror seems to be polarizing to readers, more than any other genre except maybe science fiction. There is a rabidly loyal fan base, but there also remains a large proportion of the reading public who are *sure* they could never like a horror book. Part of the gut reaction that readers may have to horror is because it is by its nature an *emotional* genre. It strives with every story to elicit a particular response. Perhaps that response is an extreme one of terror or revulsion. But dread, unease, anxiety, and fear are some of the milder emotional responses that horror can instill. What the horror averse don't realize is that the genre has got much more going on than they think. It can appeal to readers of virtually all sorts, if they look around at the variety of things that can fall under the horror umbrella. From spooky ghost stories where nary a drop of blood is spilled to all-out gore fests where you need a tarp to avoid the blood spatter, all of these are horror. Horror often deals with Evil with a capital E. It engages our primitive hindbrain that remembers both the terrors of childhood, where the shadows under the bed hold unbelievable menace, and the long-ago time when unshaped terrible things lurked in the dark where the light from our campfires ended. In the same way fantasy appeals to readers because of the echoes of fairy tales read as a child, horror calls back to the dark side of those fairy tales and the terrors that seemed so real when you were small. Real life in modern times has enough mundane horror committed by our fellow human beings; it is sometimes a release to read about horrors that are more formless and otherworldly. There is a psychological element to horror in that the monster can be metaphorical—a manifestation of psychic ills. Much of the horror that wends its way onto the "literature" shelves is psychological. But just because there is a human being at the heart of a monstrous fictional construct, that creature isn't any *less* scary— it can make it even scarier. The evil "creature" as a reflection of our basest instincts is a narrative that has a lot of power. Besides the emotional aspect of horror that manifests in the atmosphere and tone, there are other classic appeals to horror. Pacing is often a big part of why people read horror, with its steady buildup of tension and fear to a big (and often violent) climax. Characters are also important in horror in that readers cannot get an emotional response from a horror story if the authors have not made them care what happens to the characters. In the end, horror succeeds when it scares readers. And readers like to be scared for the same reason you might stick your foot out from under the covers on a freezing cold night: it feels so good when you stop. Just as readers like books about serial killers and murderers from the mystery and thriller shelves, the monsters of horror have great appeal in that one can read about them and then safely close the cover and leave those horrors on the shelf.

WHY BLEND?

Horror is a rather dominant genre, and even when it is mixed with another genre, its essential *horribleness* is often hard to ignore. To blend successfully, the qualities of horror often end up toned down, especially in the gore department. There are exceptions, of course, but one main reason that another genre is added to horror is to broaden the appeal. Books can be horrifying without being horror, of course, and just because a book scares you doesn't necessarily mean that it is horror either. The co-opting of horror staples like vampires, werewolves, and ghosts by urban fantasy and paranormal romance shows that one of the things people want to take from the horror genre is its most excellent monsters. But when the borrowed monsters are tamed and made into love interests, they lose a lot of their power to scare readers. For a blend to remain effective as a horror book, authentically scary things still need to be going on. Writers who want formerly frightening monsters as their heroes or heroines can achieve that easily by having monsters in the mix but marking them clearly as "other"—maybe there are nice vampires, but there are still *other* vampires that are decidedly not nice. But it can be difficult to pull off this kind of dichotomy, as once an author has worked hard to make a monster less scary, it's harder to make another monster strike a chord of fear. While in horror it is not unusual to have a less than happy ending—evil might triumph, good people will probably die—blending might be a way to soften this harsh lesson. Horror is not known for series because a lot of the time just about everyone is dead or the planet overrun, but when blended there are more opportunities for continuing stories.

THE BLENDS

Horror/Adrenaline

One of the genres that has absorbed some of the classic horror writers is thriller/suspense. Dean R. Koontz, John Saul, and Peter Straub were all mainstays of horror who now are found in the thriller aisles (although that doesn't mean their books have stopped having supernatural and horror elements). This is partly about marketing, of course, and a publisher trying to place its book in a way that generates the most readers and sales. But thrillers and suspense are also logical blends for horror. All are about evoking an emotional response—in fact their *names* are an emotional response! And the emotions engaged—anxiety and tension in thriller/suspense, dread and fear in horror—certainly can be tied together in our brains. A classic horror book might take a while to develop these emotional responses and might in fact deliberately draw out a scene or story to prolong the dread and fear for greater effect. A suspense book might also play with a reader's emotions to build those feelings of unease to a higher pitch. Thrillers usually take a slightly different approach in the desire to plunge readers into an emotional state and keep them there, although the escalation of mood and emotion is used to good effect as well. A reason to add a thriller or suspense aspect to a horror story is often one of pacing. While the adrenaline and horror genres both focus on building tension to a gripping climax, with adrenaline the pages tend to turn even faster because the pacing is ratcheted up.

The Atrocity Archives **by Charles Stross** (Laundry Files, book 1)

Spy fiction is a mainstay of the adrenaline genre, but what happens when you combine a spy thriller and Lovecraftian horror? You get Charles Stross's Laundry Files series. This first volume sets the stage as we are introduced to computer geek Bob Howard, who works in computer support for the Laundry, a secret governmental agency tasked with protecting Britain from the occult. Mainly a desk-bound filer of paperwork and a fixer of computer bugs, Bob is an unlikely hero, but he would love to get out in the field and prove his worth. He gets his chance when there is a threat that Nazi-summoned monsters straight out of Lovecraft might get loose in our world. In Stross's series, otherworldly, extra-dimensional powers can be tapped through technology. There's some complicated math thrown about, but as Bob explains, any science that is sufficiently advanced will look like magic to those who don't understand it. With more humor than is usual in either spy fiction or horror, Stross draws the reader in through his likeable yet smart-alecky lead. He will mostly appeal to those who will get a good UNIX joke, but the deeper Bob gets pulled into the dangerous world of eldritch spy craft the more you will pull for him. There's a lot of action squeezed into this short novel (originally serialized in magazine form), and the wicked pace helps ease readers past some of the excessive math and acronyms and British humor.

READING PATHS

If you like the elder gods and otherworldly dimensions and want horror:

The Dunwich Horror by H. P. Lovecraft

If you like the inexperienced spy dropped into the action and want a thriller:

Red Cell by Mark Henshaw

Ancestor by Scott Sigler

Scientists tinkering where they should not is a classic trope in many genres, and books with that theme often blend SF, horror, and adrenaline. The bio-thriller premise here is standard: a team of geneticists working in a remote lab are trying to find a way to create an ancestral mammalian host animal that would allow them to grow transplant organs for humans. In the high-octane opening, the US government obliterates another genetics lab that has had a security breach, then sets its sights on the Genada lab. The lab hasn't been having a lot of success, but right before the government comes to shut them down, their programmer introduces a mystery ingredient that looks like a real breakthrough. The lab staff takes its data on the run and relocates to a remote island in Lake Superior. There they implant a herd of cows with the new genotype—with disastrous results. The resulting ancestor is a deadly predator, and everyone on the island is in danger. There is some intriguing science about what we might be able to do if there were no checks on experimentation. The action never lets up, and once the predators are loose, the violence and gore factor are high enough for any horror fan. The characters, both good and bad guys, are nuanced, and if the plot is a B-movie it's one that will keep you turning pages. The novel also has an interesting backstory in that it was originally serially released as an audio podcast.

READING PATHS

If you like the medically made monster and want horror:

Breed by Chase Novak

If you like the science-run-amok plot and want a thriller:

Next by Michael Crichton

Prodigal Son by Dean R. Koontz and Kevin J. Anderson (FRANKENSTEIN, BOOK 1)

Picking up the saga of mad scientist Victor Frankenstein 200 years later could backfire with horror fans, but authors Koontz and Anderson obviously have great respect for the Frankenstein canon, both literary and cinematic. Frankenstein's original monster, now known as Deucalion, has been meditating in the Himalayan mountains for years when he discovers that his creator is improbably still alive and living in New Orleans. Frankenstein is now known as Victor Helios, and he never stopped trying to create his New Race of superbeings, intending to cleanse the earth of the inferior first draft of humans. Meanwhile NOPD detectives Carson O'Connor and Michael Maddison are tracking an apparent serial killer who is collecting body parts as trophies. Of course, the mutilations will connect back to Helios, but readers get a gripping police investigation and many intersecting monsters (both man-made and human) to complicate the story. The serial killer is a staple of thrillers, but an added thrill comes from the monstrous nature of the creatures Helios has created who are desperate to overcome their programming and the control of their hated maker. In a classic theme of horror, Helios is the most horrifying creature in the story and Deucalion the most humane, but detectives O'Connor and Maddison are a big part of why readers will keep turning pages. The only frustrating thing about this blend is that it ends with a big cliffhanger, and those wanting to find out the fate of Helios and Deucalion will need to read the rest of the series.

If you like a fresh take on the Frankenstein story and want more cerebral horror:

> *Such Wicked Intent* by Kenneth Oppel

If you like the investigator mingling with the supernatural and want a thriller:

> *The Tomb* by F. Paul Wilson

Horror/Fantasy

Horror and fantasy can be looked at as two sides of a coin. They both tend to incorporate supernatural and magic elements that seem concocted from our unconscious desires, but if fantasy is a dream, then horror is a nightmare. And let's face it—it's easy for our dreams to shift to nightmares and back again. Both genres have a heavy reliance on building a landscape for the reader, and if a fantasy world might be some place a reader would like to escape to, the horror world is one the reader will feel a palpable need to escape from—after having a goose-bump inducing look around first, of course! Descriptive language is a big part of both, as it is a tool the writer uses to put the reader into that landscape. Because so many of the monsters of horror have jumped the fence to play in the fantasy yard, there might be more crossovers in fandom than ever before. The allure of vampires or ghosts seems stronger than ever, and it is just a question of whether they still have the power to scare us. Many writers still use the monsters as a metaphor for "the other" but while Victorian horror writers might have positioned them that way to scare readers about the unknown, modern writers seem just as likely to use them as a metaphor for any outcast group. That's a pretty radical shift from "be careful of the monster" to "monsters are people too." Monster as metaphor for our own darkest impulses has been with the horror genre from the beginning. The horror monster was always likely to get hunted down and killed though, while in fantasy it may instead be tamed and domesticated. For a book to be a true blend that will appeal to a horror fan, I would propose that the monster still has to be somewhat out of control. The blends here might delight readers with their invented worlds, but they will leave them with a shiver of fear as well.

Night Watch by Sergei Lukyanenko (WATCH, BOOK 1)

What better setting for a series about the battles between Dark and Light than Moscow in the gritty early years of the post-Soviet era? In Lukyanenko's series, which begins with *Night Watch*, there are two opposing forces of Others, the Night Watch on the side of the Light and the Day Watch who follow the Dark. The two groups keep an uneasy truce, their purpose to make sure the other side does not interfere with humans by swaying them to one side or the other. In this first volume, we follow Night Watch analyst Anton through three connected stories. Employing a classic urban fantasy technique, his world is our world but with choices and creatures invisible to the uninitiated. What ties the three stories together, besides the wonderful character of Anton who is used and abused by both his employers and their enemies, is the moral ambiguity of the supposedly simple dichotomy. Shape-shifters, vampires, and magicians of the light and dark variety are all tools in the war for the souls of humanity that has been raging for centuries. No one does bleak like the Russians, and the struggle of good against evil has rarely been done darker.

READING PATHS

If you like a war between good and evil for the souls of humanity and want horror:

Swan Song by Robert McCammon

If you like the Russian sensibility and want fantasy:

The Stranger by Max Frei

Neverwhere by Neil Gaiman

Mild-mannered everyman Richard Mayhew is going about his life, complete with a good job and beautiful fiancée, when he encounters the strange girl known as Door. He finds her bleeding on a London street and impulsively takes her to his home to recuperate. The next day, two very menacing not-quite-right men are at his door, looking for the girl. Using Door's magical powers to create openings where she needs them, the two escape to a frightening and surreal mirror of London called London Below, and Richard will not be able to return to his old life until he helps Door complete her quest. They are aided by the tricky Marquis de Carabas and hunted by Mr. Croup and Mr.

Vandermar, whose conversations are by turns hilarious and deeply chilling. Underground, Richard encounters angels and monsters and must face down darkness around him and find courage he never knew he had. All of Gaiman's books, from the *Sandman* graphic novel series onward, have a touch of the dark side of a bedtime story. There are magic and beauty in his worlds, but danger and darkness are always there too. He might be the best example of an author able to yoke the wonder of fantasy with the foreboding of horror in a way that will make you shiver, even if you won't be sure whether it is a shiver of delight or fear.

READING PATHS

If you like the journey through a dark mirror London and want horror:

King Rat by China Miéville

If you like the darker tone and the quest through different worlds and want fantasy:

Imajica by Clive Barker

Sunshine by Robin McKinley

Straddling the line between horror and urban fantasy, *Sunshine* tells the story of the basically cheerful Rae "Sunshine" Seddon who enjoys a quiet life working in her stepfather's bakery. One night she wanders too far from home and is attacked and kidnapped by a gang of vampires. She wakes up in a decrepit mansion at the edge of town, chained to a wall. And she's not alone—the gang has chained her up with a half-starved vampire named Constantine. The two form a tentative bond and when Sunshine remembers a trick her grandmother taught her to tap her dormant magic, they both escape. When it is obvious that the vampires will be after them both, Sunshine and Con decide to work together. The tone is by turns light and dark: very funny internal monologues and scenes of everyday life mixed with very dark, menacing horror. The obvious fan base for *Sunshine* is those who loved the TV series *Buffy the Vampire Slayer*, with its mix of perky and determined heroine, sympathetic vampire, and really dangerous supernatural threats. Con no doubt has a pull on Sunshine, but this is not a fluffy romance, and there are no neat happy endings to this story. No wonder McKinley's fans have been begging for a sequel since this came out!

READING PATHS

If you like the alliance between a human and vampires and want horror:

Those Who Hunt the Night by Barbara Hambly

If you like the story of a young woman discovering her own power in a dark fantasy:

Darkfever by Karen Marie Moning

Horror/Historical

Because the emotional response in horror is rooted in the readers being able to put themselves into the story, adding a historical frame would appear to make that more difficult. But when it is done well, historical fiction can be utterly transporting and this difficulty melts away. A good horror story, as long as it is built on the strong bones of making you empathize with the characters and experience the frightening things with them, can happen in any time. The historical period can actually add to the experience of reading horror. Unlike our own time period in which we know the rules and the environment around us, historical fiction's frame is deliberately not our own. People living in earlier times knew less about their own world than we do now and might have been more likely to label the unknown as supernatural. They also seemed to live closer to their fears, without the veneer of modern civilization, and these historical superstitions and fears can be great fodder for horror. Historical characters tend to be more ready to believe that there are monsters in the world, so authors don't need to the spend time required to overcome a modern protagonist's desire to rationalize the unknown. Having a setting that we don't know so well adds an exotic element that goes down well with horror. It pushes readers out of their comfort zone, which is exactly where a horror writer wants them to be.

Dead of Winter by Brian Moreland

The untamed wilderness at the edges of settled lands is a great setting for a historical horror novel. Everything about the setting is hostile, from the primitive conditions to the killing cold. Fort Pendleton is deep in the Ontario frontier, and its isolation and remoteness leave the residents vulnerable to not only the brutal winters but also a terrifying supernatural menace. Inspector Tom Hatcher is investigating a plague that has beset the fort, turning victims into cannibalistic flesh eaters. Meanwhile in Quebec, a Catholic priest visits a jailed serial killer captured years earlier by Hatcher. The two men must work together when they realize that demonic forces are at work. The historical setting of 1870s Canada is drawn with a special attention to the difficulties of life on the rough frontier. The delicate relations with local native tribes like the Ojibwa add to the accuracy of the historical setting, as well as adding another layer to the supernatural elements at play. Ranging from spooky to scary to bloody as hell, the horror in *Dead of Winter* builds and adds tension until the violent demonic confrontation at the end.

READING PATHS

If you like the violent story of demonic possession and want more horror:

Cold Fire by Dean R. Koontz

If you like the Canadian frontier setting and want more historical fiction:

The Holding by Merilyn Simonds

Something Red by Douglas Nicholas (SOMETHING RED, BOOK 1)

Something is hunting travelers in the far North of England. Hob is a 12-year-old traveling 13th-century Britain in the company of an exiled Irish queen known by the English as Molly, her granddaughter Nemain, and Jack Brown, their phlegmatic companion. The group stops in a monastery high in a mountain pass, but violence visits the sanctuary in the form of a monk brutally eviscerated by some unknown beast. They continue to encounter violence and bad weather after they leave the monastery and must shelter within the strong defenses of a nearby castle. Unfortunately, it looks like the beast they have been tracking is locked in with them. The details of life in medieval England, from the clothing and food to the details of castle life, all paint an incredibly vivid picture. In less skilled hands, the descriptions of meals, for instance, might have seemed like a writer showing off his research. But Nicholas is a poet, and his descriptions of such mundane things as Hob's handling of his beloved ox make this a book that transports readers completely. Molly is a fascinating character, mysterious and powerful, but every member of the company will cast a spell. Each incident of violence, despite not being very graphic in description, adds to the tension of this page-turner, in which the final confrontation is a welcome relief from the buildup of pressure.

READING PATHS

If you like the medieval setting and want more horror:

Mister B. Gone by Clive Barker

If you like the journey through a medieval England and want more historical fiction:

Company of Liars by Karen Maitland

Twelve by Jasper Kent (DANILOV QUINTET, BOOK 1)

War can be an ideal backdrop for horror, as the reader is usually prepared to encounter inhuman acts of cruelty and bloodshed. How interesting then to add an additional level of inhuman violence that takes the reader by surprise. In *Twelve*, Jasper Kent chooses the fascinating historical setting of the Napoleonic Wars and an even more unusual perspective of the Russian side of those campaigns. Aleksei Ivanovich Danilov is a captain in the Russian army and an expert in covert espionage behind enemy lines. The war is not going so well for Russia, and as Aleksei meets up with three comrade spies, he learns that one of them has hired a group of 12 mercenaries to help turn the tide. The 12 fighters, called *oprichniki*, make Aleksei nervous from the beginning, but they leave a path of destruction in their wake that is hard to argue against. It is only when he realizes that the *oprichniki* are vampires, feeding on French and Russians alike in their thirst for blood, that Aleksei decides they must be stopped. The details of the advance of Napoleon's forces toward Moscow help to ground the story without boring those uninterested in war stories. Aleksei is a conflicted character, a little navel-gazey and obsessed with his local mistress (despite having a loving wife back in Petersburg), but he remains a sympathetic, if conflicted, hero. The vampiric *oprichniki* are a great villainous force on the stage, merciless and with only the thinnest veneer of humanity over their monstrous urges.

READING PATHS

If you like the 19th-century historical setting and want more vampire horror:

Fevre Dream by George R. R. Martin

If you like the setting of the Russian invasion during the Napoleonic Wars and want historical fiction:

The Retreat by Patrick Rambaud

Horror/Mystery

There is often at least a hint of a mystery in horror, even if it comes in the form of a puzzle whose question is not "who done it?" but "what the heck is going on here?!" There is usually something unexplained in horror, and although the narrative can simply be a person or group reacting to that thing, the best horror spends at least some time trying to explore the nature of a supernatural something. In a horror/mystery blend, that exploration might lean on the mystery formula to become an actual investigation. The mystery genre does, after all, usually have something terrible and arguably unnatural at its heart: murder. The very act of a character being killed can be the thing that kicks off a mystery, but it might also be the opening act of a horror novel. Both genres are often rooted in violence, but how they portray that violence often sets them apart. Of course, mysteries can be quite genteel in their handling of dead bodies, but even in a darker mystery there are usually lines that are not crossed in the description of violence, and curtains drawn across the most horrible acts. But horror doesn't obey those lines, and it pulls back the curtain. It revels in showing the dark things—both around us and inside us. The darker tone and feeling of dread that are hallmarks of horror, when applied to a mystery formula, can work quite well. The need to punish the guilty and rescue the innocent, so often core to a mystery, doesn't always translate to horror blends, however. Horror has always been comfortable with the idea that evil is eternal and the innocent often suffer. Mystery readers who like a tidy justice-filled resolution might not get the closure they are looking for.

Last Days by Brian Evenson

Although the supernatural is a hallmark of many classics of horror, sometimes the horrible things can be our fellow man. Another dominant characteristic of the genre is a certain amount of gleeful mutilation and gore, and *Last Days* delivers up gore galore. Evenson sets up his story as a classic mystery, with former undercover cop Kline recruited by some very odd characters to investigate a crime in a religious cult. He is chosen because he lost his hand during his last investigation for the police. The narrative quickly turns surreal as he starts asking questions of the cult members, who all view the cutting off of body parts as a way to experience religious ecstasy. This group is so secretive that they refuse to tell Kline the details of the crime before he joins their higher ranks and cuts off a few more body parts. The amputations are vivid but strangely clinical as well, and the escalation of violence is classic horror. But through it all, Kline doggedly keeps trying to get to the bottom of the supposed crime within the group, even if it costs him his pound of flesh. The mystery provides a good entry into the story, although it will not prove entirely satisfying as a puzzle. A better match for this is a fan of Kafka-esque surreal horror, but one who has an appreciation of suspenseful noir.

READING PATHS

For more horror in which the evil is entirely and creepily human:

Neuropath by R. Scott Bakker

If you like the investigator going down the rabbit hole and want a mystery:

Every Dead Thing by John Connolly

The Chosen Child by Graham Masterton

There is a monster loose in the sewers of Warsaw, cutting people's heads off and retreating back to the tunnels. This is bad news for Sarah Leonards, who is trying to get a luxury hotel built in the city, when some of her workers are killed during excavation work for the building. The victims often heard a child crying before something rushed out of the darkness to strike. When the workers on her hotel site think there is a demon on the loose and refuse to continue on the project, Sarah works with a Warsaw police detective named Stefan Rej to find out what connects the victims of this truly scary menace. This is a classic odd-couple sleuthing scenario, but the unusual setting and character building make it worth seeking out. The investigation delves into corporate finances and Poland's dark WWII past for a gripping mystery. But it is the tension brought by the unknown but implacable nature of the sewer-dwelling menace and the gruesome speed and brutality of his killing that show why Masterson is a core writer in the horror genre.

READING PATHS

If you like the monster living in the sewers and want horror:

It by Stephen King

If you like a crime that gets blamed on a monster and want a mystery:

The Bedlam Detective by Stephen Gallagher

The Frenzy Way **by Gregory Lamberson (FRENZY CYCLE, BOOK 1)**

Much of the time when an author mixes another genre with horror the end result (if not the intention) is to tone down the violence, lessen the gore factor, and make the book more palatable to other fandoms. Lamberson's series featuring NYPD detective Anthony Mace has plenty of violence, blood, and gore for a horror reader, while still having the solid bones of a mystery. Mace has recently been promoted at the beginning of *The Frenzy Way*, when he catches a particularly horrendous case. Bodies have been found that show signs of evisceration by some kind of animal. One of those bodies was a college professor who studies werewolf myths. Mace begins to believe that the killer is supernatural in nature, but the rest of the NYPD think they are dealing with a serial killer. There are other forces interested in solving the crime as well, including a Native American tribal policeman, an occult bookstore owner, and a priest. The mixture of folklore, religion, and werewolves that are genuinely *scary* make this a departure from the urban fantasy creatures. In a way the book passes through the two genres as the story unfolds, and each is handled with skill: a police procedural opening as the cops investigate and the killer is revealed, accelerating into an action-packed bloody horror climax. The strong characterization and exploration of werewolf mythology makes this a winning blend.

READING PATHS

If you like the werewolf as bad guy and want more horror:

The Sticks by Andy Deane

If you like the police investigation of the supernatural and want a mystery:

A Matter of Blood by Sarah Pinborough

Horror/Romance

If ever there seemed to be two genres that should never be found together it would be romance (the genre of happy, loving endings) and horror (the bloody bastion of monsters that will eat your face). But sex, certainly, has been a part of horror from the beginning. Whether through the Victorian warnings about excessive sensuality with a supernatural bow on it (Bram Stoker's *Dracula*) or the cliché found in countless teen horror flicks that the girl who has sex is the first to die, horror has always included books that linked sex and violence. But *love*, now that's a different kettle of fish.

It's certainly not impossible to have a love story in horror. There are many, many paranormal romances out there that use the creatures from horror literature but make them intriguing alpha-type romantic objects. While some of these still manage to have some scares in them, by domesticating the monsters, an author has probably stepped away from horror. A typical horror plot might have a lone man facing supernatural evil, but what changes when you take the lone man and add the woman he loves? If the desire to be with and protect loved ones is a core human trait, what could be more natural than to protect them from a horde of ravening zombies? Giving a protagonist a loved one to be with in the midst of a horror plot not only adds dimension and sympathy to that protagonist, but it also makes the stakes even higher. Readers want the hero or heroine to survive the story, but they also want to imagine them happy in the end. Happily ever after is what romance is all about. But to get to a happy ending that has meaning, characters have to go through conflict. And it's hard to imagine a bigger conflict than a monster trying to eat your face off.

The Restorer by Amanda Stevens (THE GRAVEYARD QUEEN, BOOK 1)

Cemetery restorer Amelia Gray has lived her life in the shadow of her ability to see ghosts. From her father, she learned the rules that keep her safe, the most important being to never look at or acknowledge a ghost or she will never be free of it. After Amelia stumbles upon a dead body of the fresh variety in the Charleston cemetery she has been hired to restore, she encounters Charleston Police Detective Devlin, who would be right up Amelia's alley if not for the ghost of his wife and child that follow him around town. The question becomes whether she can help him solve the murder without losing her own life. The genres that mix together in *The Restorer* all take center stage at different points in the narrative, making this a book you could offer many different readers. There is a mystery structure (bonus genre!) to the plot that keeps the pages turning as the bodies accumulate and the danger quotient goes up. But the horror elements add lots of layers of creepy, menacing atmosphere that make you scared to turn the pages. The romantic angle adds enough attraction to interest paranormal romance readers who are willing to compromise on a perfectly happy ending. But at its heart, this is a book about a woman trying to control a supernatural force that is intent on destroying her and any chance at her happiness.

READING PATHS

If you like ghost stories and want more horror:

Her Fearful Symmetry by Audrey Niffenegger

If you like ghost stories and want more paranormal romance:

The House on Tradd Street by Karen White

The Haunting of Maddy Clare by Simone St. James

In 1920s England, Sarah Piper is sent by a temporary employment agency on a rather unusual assignment to assist ghost hunter Alistair Gellis. Gellis is a WWI vet who writes rather dry books about hauntings around Britain. He and Sarah head out, along with mysterious ghost-hunting assistant Matthew Ryder, to investigate a phenomenon at a country barn. The ghost of Maddy Clare is haunting the place where she committed suicide and, according to her former employer, has a special antipathy for men. It is up to Sarah, then, to make contact. She does and is quickly overwhelmed by Maddy's spirit who demands that they find the men who wronged her or she will kill Alistair. Matthew and Sarah work closely together to find out what really happened to Maddy, and a strong attraction grows between them. The powerful and vengeful spirit is done well, and the tension builds as they race to stop Maddy in time. Although Sarah and Matthew's relationship has a troubled beginning (Matthew and Alistair have both been greatly affected by their wartime experiences), it builds nicely. There are some lovely historical touches (bonus genre!) about the long shadow cast on England by WWI, but the story mostly works because of the great character of Sarah, who is vulnerable but with untapped strength.

READING PATHS

If you like the ghost-hunter plot and want more gothic horror:

The Woman in Black by Susan Hill

If you like the gothic feel but want more of a romance:

The Bride Finder by Susan Carroll

Allison Hewitt Is Trapped by **Madeleine Roux**

With its structure of blog entries collected many years after the outbreak of a zombie plague, this first novel really did first begin on the author's blog as an experiment in serial fiction narrative. It tells the story of bookstore clerk Allison Hewitt and her efforts to survive the zombie apocalypse. After initially holing up in her bookstore, Allison ends up at the football stadium on campus (the book appears to be set in Madison, Wisconsin) where the city's survivors have gathered. There she meets Collin, the charismatic leader of the stadium survivors, and they find comfort in each other as the danger escalates. Then, against all odds, Collin's presumed-dead wife shows up at the stadium and Allison decides to go back on the run. There is some gruesome zombie action throughout the book, but it is not extreme and certainly less than most works in this genre. As is often the case in good horror, there are evil creatures both inhuman and human to contend against. The character of Allison is the pull for this book, which reads like an unlikely but successful blend of zombie horror and chick lit. Allison is trying to survive the apocalypse, yes, but she is also trying to find herself *and* she's hoping to have a real connection with someone in the midst of the horror. The structure of the book as a series of blog entries is effective, as we get a full picture of the apocalyptic world from the comments left by fellow survivors who find Allison's blog. While not for hard-core zombie fans, this look at the apocalypse still manages to pack in tense action and scares.

READING PATHS

If you like the zombie action but want something darker from horror:

Dead of Night by Jonathan Maberry

If you like the zombies but want more romance:

Dearly, Departed by Lia Habel

Horror/Science Fiction

Two genres that don't seem to have a lot of common ground are horror and science fiction. Science fiction is an intellectual genre, interested in the future and investigating where we are going and focused heavily on science and technology. Horror, by contrast, is all emotion and thrives in the shadowy corners of the things we don't know, with a backbone in ancient evils and things that go bump in the night. But if you strip away the set decoration and focus on the mood and atmosphere used to such great effect in horror, those elements can be blended with science fiction for some seriously scary results. Some interesting and terrifying things can happen in fiction when science pokes its nose in places that should have been left alone. There are three basic ways a writer can inject an SF vibe into a horror story. One is to set the story in the future. The basic premise can still have that supernatural edge, but if the setting is convincingly futuristic, you will get some crossover love. Another is to have your supernatural menace be birthed from the antiseptic loins of science: a plague escaped from the lab, a genetically engineered monstrosity, or an evolutionary quirk with terrifying consequences. Finally, the big bad thing everyone is running from is from outer space. The monster-as-alien, if done well, can be just as terrifying as the monster-from-the-unknown. What's more unknown than outer space, after all? Adding some SF to horror can bring a literal otherworldly nature to the menace, and it can also provide a good contrast. If SF involves the intellect, horror often short-circuits intellectual thought in favor of emotion. Starting from a super-logical SF place and devolving into a terror-filled emotional response can be a great narrative journey.

Invasion of the Body Snatchers by **Jack Finney**

SF films are chock full of horrifying space aliens. One of the iconic alien encounters in fiction was originally simply called *The Body Snatchers*, but after being filmed multiple times, the movie name stuck. The book is as scary as any of the film versions, with alien seeds invading Earth by drifting down and replacing sleeping humans with "pod people." Dr. Miles Bennell starts getting reports from patients that their friends and loved ones look the same but are somehow not themselves. Miles dismisses this as hysteria until a trusted friend brings him irrefutable truth that aliens are growing duplicates in creepy vegetative pods. When Miles's childhood sweetheart, Becky, is almost swapped for her alien duplicate, the two end up on the run. A slim book that packs a lot of action into its pages, the version republished in 1978 updates some of the story elements from its original release in the 1950s. The SF elements are effective in the way the story takes a new look at the alien as "other" even if they lack a certain depth (such as the reasoning behind the alien invasion and eventual retreat). But the tension, the dread of knowing your loved ones are not what they seem, makes this a great study in paranoia. The idiom of "pod people" has stuck with us through the decades because of how creepily horrible it is to imagine people replaced with emotionless aliens bent on taking over the planet.

READING PATHS

If you like the doppelgängers and want more horror:

The Dark Half by Stephen King

If you like the alien invasion and want more SF:

The Puppet Masters by Robert A. Heinlein

Feed by Mira Grant (NEWSFLESH, BOOK 1)

Mira Grant tells a tale, set in the year 2039, of a world that has reached a certain equilibrium 25 years after a lab-engineered virus that was meant to cure the common cold instead caused a zombie outbreak that nearly destroyed society. The zombies are still out there, and humanity has retreated to defensible compounds. Siblings Shaun and Georgia Mason, along with their friend and tech expert Buffy, are in the news business, which these days is dominated by bloggers. They are attached to the presidential campaign of Senator Peter Ryman, an idealistic politician whose campaign suddenly sees an uptick in zombie attacks. However, these attacks may not be the usual random zombie violence, but a concerted assault by a political enemy. The action is intense in this opening volume of the series, both with the zombies and the nail-biting suspense of a political thriller (bonus genre!). Georgia is the narrator and heart of the book, tough but devoted to two things: her brother and the integrity of their news blog. The zombie attacks are vicious and scary, but the real achievement in *Feed* is the world that Grant has built. It is a great SF setting, in which she really makes readers think about what life would be like under the constant threat of viral contamination. Another nifty bit of speculation here is about the possible future of news reporting, positing that only social media would be nimble enough to deal with a crisis. For a new take on a standard horror monster, Grant's Newsflesh trilogy shows that there is still life in the undead.

READING PATHS

If you like the social media take on a zombie outbreak but want more gory horror:

Midnight Movie by Tobe Hooper

If you like a more scientific take on a zombie virus and want SF:

Aftertime by Sophie Littlefield

I Am Legend by Richard Matheson

There have been scientific takes on a lot of different monsters from the horror toy box, but vampires seem so rooted in the Judeo-Christian tradition of demons and souls that most writers like to keep the origins of vampirism safely in the mythology zone. One of the first (and still one of the best) books to imagine vampirism as caused by a plague is the short novel *I Am Legend*. In it we get a vivid postapocalyptic landscape in which Robert Neville is the sole survivor of a pandemic that has turned every other human into blood-craving, sun-shunning monsters. The horror setting is well drawn, with Neville barricaded in his home, despairing in his belief that he is the very last human on the planet. Obsessed with finding the cause for this disease to which he is somehow immune, Neville scours scientific tomes and performs experiments on the vampires both dead and alive. He's perfected his technique for killing the vampires when he suddenly comes upon Ruth, another apparently uninfected survivor. The matter-of-fact way that Neville tells his story is almost documentary in nature. His scientific approach to understanding and killing the infected is effective, but what if it's based on a faulty premise? Much of the power of this work comes from the character of Neville, who shuttles between emotional extremes of despondency and determination. Without spoiling anything, this has one of the most powerful endings that will change how you view everything that came before.

READING PATHS

If you like the dark picture of a man alone at the end of the world and want horror:

The Return Man by V. M. Zito

If you like the postapocalyptic landscape but want SF:

Domino Falls by Steven Barnes and Tananarive Due

WORKING WITH HORROR BLENDS

If you don't know that a reader is already a fan of horror (or sometimes even if you do), the key to finding a good blend is to know her limits. Does she like to be scared? How scared? Is blood OK? If we are talking about a trickle versus a bucket of blood, does that change the answer? How about disemboweling? Too far? Just as with romance recommendations you probably want to get a sense of how graphic your reader likes things in terms of details, the same goes for horror. You can open a reader up to the horror genre with the right blend, but it helps if you prepare the way by letting her know what to expect. The level of gore and disturbing imagery is variable in horror as a whole, as well as with the blends. You can always find something that leans toward the tamer side of things in terms of violence if you get a sense that your reader is not comfortable with a lot of blood and guts. But remember that it is not only the violence that people react to with horror and horror blends. There are people who find the buildup of tension that is common in horror very appealing. The sensation that you can't bear to see what happens next but you can't wait until you find out what happens next is a common push/pull in the emotional genres, but in horror it has the added dimension of evoking real fear. There are readers who just can't take that level of tension in their books. A blend can often soften the "boo/eek" jolts that leave readers of horror unsettled. But the bottom line is that the reader has to *want* to be scared, at least a little, for a horror blend to work. Once you know that he is willing to take a little walk on the dark side, let the scaring begin.

5

MYSTERY BLENDS
Blends with a Puzzle

A mystery can be roughly defined as a story in which a crime has been committed and someone investigates to find out how and why that crime occurred. The crime in a mystery is often murder, but it need not always be. Any wrongdoing engaging enough to readers that they have a real and undeniable desire to find out "who done it" will do. The typical opening act for a mystery plot is the introduction of a cast of characters, the discovery of a crime, and the identification of an investigator. This opening can have a lot of variation such as with police procedurals, in which the investigator might be on stage first. After the crime is committed, the second act can commence, which involves identifying a pool of suspects, the presentation of clues, and a variety of impediments, complications, and escalating conflicts. Some mysteries pride themselves on giving readers the chance to figure out the guilty party along with the investigator, and they give readers all the same clues to solve the puzzle. Other writers will toy more with readers, dropping misleading clues or withholding crucial information to provide a more shocking ending. The final act of any mystery involves the solving of the crime and the punishment of the guilty. This might seem like a predictable formula, but there are thousands of ways to tell a story that include these elements. In addition, a shared investigative backbone doesn't mean all mysteries read the same. As in most genres, there is a plethora of subgenres to be found. In mystery, most subgenres are defined by the identity of their protagonists: police procedurals, private investigators, amateur sleuths, and so on. Even within those categories, there are variations in appeal that mean that, for mystery, one size does not fit all. From cozy to hard-boiled, from light and humorous to gritty and noir, there is a mystery to suit most reading tastes. When blending, an author can play with this formula, but readers must still be able to recognize the genre conventions to appreciate when an author has strayed from them.

APPEAL OF MYSTERY

Not only are mysteries consistently a huge part of the best-seller lists, they are some of the highest circulating titles at our libraries. But why? Part of the appeal is that mysteries allow us to visit a world where terrible things happen . . . to other people. You get a chance as a reader to hear about a crime and get caught up in the chase for a killer, but all from the safety of your comfy couch. With many genres, you are reading to visit a world or situation that offers wish fulfillment. Conversely, there can be great reader satisfaction in vicariously visiting a scary world filled with crime or violence. It can put our own problems into perspective and give us a really satisfying sense of closure due to the element of justice usually found in the stories. Whether the crime is little or big, the perpetrators usually get caught and the guilty punished. This formula with its predictable end-game can be as comforting to a reader of mysteries as the happily ever after can be to romance readers. In our real lives, injustices are not always righted and the guilty get away with monstrous wrongs. So isn't it satisfying to have things turn out better in a book?

Mysteries have an added appeal of being engaging puzzles. The reader is usually in the dark along with the detective and can be an active participant in the process of considering clues, discarding red herrings, and guessing who will end up being the guilty party. In this important sense, traditional mysteries differ from their near kin in the adrenaline genres, especially the suspense and thriller novels. In adrenaline books, there might also be a crime, but the psychology of the crime and the suspense of whether or not it will be thwarted are more important than veiling the villain from the reader, and pacing can be more central to their appeal than it is in mysteries. The importance of the puzzle to your readers will be a major part of finding them a good blend, as the rules can get bent in service to another genre.

Story elements like the puzzle may be what most readers think about when they picture books in this genre, but characters are central to the appeal of mysteries as well. The reader must almost always be engaged in the story through an empathetic bond with the protagonist (usually the investigator) to care about the outcome. The appeal of character is one reason why series books are so core to the mystery genre. Although there have been countless wonderful stand-alone mystery stories, many of the most popular feature recurring characters. The appeal of the series in mysteries is that you usually have a completely new story arc every time, but you get to revisit characters you have grown attached to. In a golden age mystery series like the Hercule Poirot books, the Belgian detective doesn't show a lot of personal growth from book to book, but his very stability and sameness draw readers back. In other series, the development of the character over time is part of why fans keep coming back. In many acclaimed mysteries, such as those of P. D. James, the character investigations are as intriguing as the criminal ones, and the reader gains insights into the human psyche.

WHY BLEND?

If mysteries are already one of the most popular genres in publishing, why mess with success and blend in another genre? Because the mystery genre has a heavy reliance on formula, the books can seem predictable. The structure of the story arc with the crime, investigation, and solution are so core to the genre that they can lead to monotony when taken in large doses over multiple books. Adding another genre shakes things up, plays with expectations, and makes the reading experience a little more unpredictable even as the backbone of the story remains familiar. In some blends, the genre mixed in will add an interesting and exotic frame. Historical fiction, science fiction, and fantasy can easily be used this way. A murder . . . in space! A crime spree . . . in Victorian England! This change of venue can add interest while leaving the formula more or less intact. Other blends use the strengths of their genre to change how a book is experienced by the reader, such as an atmosphere of heightened dread with horror or an increase in the tension and pacing with adrenaline.

In examining books that have been blended with mysteries, I looked for titles that still have an interesting puzzle at their center. In the suggestions that follow, I've chosen books that I think exemplify ways mystery can be blended with other genres so that they still please mystery readers but may also attract others to the genre—and may also lead mystery readers outside their crime-scene-taped comfort zones. Whether marketed to mystery fans or beyond readers of that genre, these titles build on the mystery fan base, but they may also be of interest to a wider audience.

THE BLENDS

Mystery/Adrenaline

In fiction there are some genres that are naturally kissing cousins, and how you decide to classify a book comes down to nuance and marketing decisions. This is nowhere truer than in the borderlands between mystery and adrenaline genres, such as thriller and suspense. Looking at many of the most popular authors in mystery, you will see different labels on their books over time, sometimes even within a particular series. Sometimes authors will be marketed as mystery early on, but as they gain a following and get more of a marketing push, their publishers will drop the "mystery" designation on the cover. One example is the Goldy Bear books by Diane Mott Davidson. The first in the series, *Catering to Nobody*, came out with "A Murder Mystery" prominently on the cover. The latest entries have a much smaller bit of text on the bottom of the cover reading "A Novel of Suspense." This desire to de-genrify a book was discussed in Chapter 1 and is usually rooted in the publisher's desire to broaden the appeal of a book beyond the genre's core readers. Marketing decisions aside, there are differences between mysteries and adrenaline novels.

If a mystery is about what happens after a crime, an adrenaline title is often about what happens before the crime. A mystery tries to find a killer, but adrenaline is just as likely to focus on preventing a killing. An actual mystery/adrenaline blend is one in which the focus remains on the central puzzle but appeal aspects of adrenaline are layered in, usually pacing and a shift from a tight focus on the protagonist and investigation. In some blends a crime is committed but the protagonist is racing to prevent further bloodshed or trying not to become the next victim. This shift in focus retains the puzzle-solving of a mystery but adds the tension and anticipation of possible violence that mark adrenaline reads. The blurring of the line between mysteries and adrenaline, especially in the suspense subgenre, is a natural consequence of mysteries moving beyond their early roots, with the spotlight on the investigations to find out who the killer is, to the more nuanced focus on motive and the psychology of crime found more in today's mysteries. If one of the basic tenets of mystery is to hide the identity of the killer until the big reveal at the end, a mystery/adrenaline blend will often bend that a little. This can be done by adding the viewpoint of the killer as a non-primary narrator, breaking from the traditional first-person narration found in most mysteries in which the reader usually does not know more than the protagonist. Another way these blends differ from most mysteries is in the stakes at risk. If a mystery is about one person dying, a thriller is just as likely to be about preventing a stadium full of people from dying. So when you take the more cerebral puzzle of a mystery and add a touch of the brawnier action of a thriller, you get a faster read and some of the emotional highs and lows of an adrenaline read.

Sleepyhead by Mark Billingham (TOM THORNE, BOOK 1)

Books like *Sleepyhead* combine some of the tricks of a thriller with a classic police procedural. Tom Thorne is a world-weary middle-aged cop in London who finds himself investigating a murder spree in which it is believed that the killer eventually screwed up and left a victim alive, if in a coma. But what if he wanted his victims in a coma and the first three deaths were mistakes? Serial killer books are more often found in the adrenaline territory where the focus is on preventing future violence, but the detailed immersion into the world of police investigation puts this book firmly in the mystery camp as well. Each chapter begins with the narrative voice of the killer, another technique more often found in thrillers than mysteries. The complicated characters, moral ambiguities, plot twists, and dark tone are what make this and other Billingham books standout blends. The pacing and accelerating tensions as well as a climax with many lives on the line are all hallmarks of a great thriller. Yet the story of a careworn cop doggedly pursuing the criminal, and the fact that it is the first book of a series, mean that this will work well for mystery readers too.

READING PATHS

If you like the doggedly determined but depressive detective and want a mystery:

The Black Echo by Michael Connelly

If you like the law enforcement protagonist and serial killer on the loose and want a thriller:

Birdman by Mo Hayder

In the Woods by Tana French (DUBLIN MURDER SQUAD, BOOK 1)

Psychological suspense and mystery can be found mixing happily on both our mystery and fiction shelves. One of the best examples of mysteries that always feature a huge helping of psychological suspense is the Dublin Murder Squad series from Tana French, starting with *In the Woods*. The series focuses on different cases and detectives each time, but all share a strong sense of place and some recurring characters. *In the Woods* begins when Dublin detective Ryan Roberts and his partner catch a career-making case involving a missing girl. But the psychological tension is ratcheted up by the fact that Ryan was involved in a horrifyingly similar case when he was a child in that same neighborhood. There are twists and turns to appeal to the thriller reader, but French also spends a lot of time on showing readers inside the minds of these cops and their motivations. With an elegant writing style that gives a good sense of place, *In the Woods* is a police procedural that is as much about the scars left by childhood trauma and the cost of secrets as it is about finding the criminal.

READING PATHS

If you like the emphasis on character motivations, twisty plots, and polished prose and want a mystery:

The Private Patient by P. D. James

If you like unreliable narrators and dark psychological suspense but want a thriller:

Half Broken Things by Morag Joss

Think of a Number by John Verdon (DAVE GURNEY, BOOK 1)

The retired detective lured back to the game for one last irresistible case is a trope found throughout the mystery genre. (Laurie R. King's fabulous series about Sherlock Holmes's post-retirement escapades is but one example.) In Verdon's series featuring recently retired "supercop" Dave Gurney, we get a book that is an example of the über-puzzle: a mystery so impossible to solve that only the legendary Gurney will do. He is brought into the case initially by an old friend who received a mysterious letter saying, "Think of any number . . . picture it . . . now see how well I know your secrets." When a subsequent letter arrives with the correct number inside, both the reader and the detective will be compelled to figure out how the trick was done, especially when the friend ends up dead. With a focus on complex, fascinating characters, a compelling villain who remains tantalizingly offstage, and a truly engaging puzzle, this first book in a series will appeal to those who enjoy the intellectual aspects of traditional mysteries but want the breakneck pacing and psychological delving of a thriller.

READING PATHS

If you like a retired detective who can't resist the chase being brought back for a difficult case and would like a mystery:

New York Dead by Stuart Woods

If you like the cat-and-mouse game, full of tension and a battle of intellects, and want a thriller:

Devotion of Suspect X by Keigo Higashino

Mystery/Fantasy

As was discussed in the chapter on fantasy, a huge part of that genre falls into the subfamily of urban fantasy, which has a heavy crossover with mystery. The degree to which crime-centric urban fantasies will appeal to a core mystery fan varies and can come down to how willing a reader is to suspend disbelief. If readers have an aversion to anything they cannot imagine actually happening to them (even if they picture it with dread), then a blend with fantasy is probably not a good bet. However, for those intrigued by stories of myth and magic, these blends can offer rich rewards. Fantasy as a genre has a strong focus on frame—the world building, magic systems, and the basic look and feel of a fantasy are a huge part of why readers in the genre keep coming back. There is also often a quest or struggle between light and dark in fantasy story lines, with characters striving to defeat evil (big E or little). When authors add the touch of myth, the twist of strange, or the striving against a bigger Evil to a mystery, it raises the stakes for readers and plays against expectations. However, the larger the dose of fantasy, the greater the challenge it is to put the books into the hands of traditional mystery fans. The focus here is on books that are still recognizably crime novels at their hearts but that borrow elements from fantasy. Like with romance, fantasy is a genre that appeals more to a reader's emotions than intellect, so authors of blends must usually choose whom they are aiming to please. If an author provides an interesting enough puzzle, readers might just go along with the fantasy elements. Fantasy can bring a valuable sense of wonder and imagination to what is otherwise a very grounded genre.

Storm Front by Jim Butcher (DRESDEN FILES, BOOK 1)

A more seamless blend of mystery and fantasy would be hard to find than the early books of the urban fantasy series featuring wizard Harry Dresden. Jim Butcher has created a recognizable, present-day Chicago, where real magic exists without average joes ever realizing it. Harry is a powerful magician and, like a modern-day version of a fairy tale knight, he is errant, chivalrous, always fighting for the little guy, defending the weak, and risking his life for his friends and the wider world. But in a thoroughly winning combo, he is also a classic noir detective, investigating crimes, fighting for the little guy, risking his . . . hey—those two things actually go together really well! While books in the series vary widely in their balance between magic and mystery, the earlier entries can be seen as classic private investigator mysteries in which our hero simply substitutes spells for forensics and a magic staff for a gun. This doesn't mean that there isn't some great world building for fantasy fans: a council of wizards governing the magic wielders of the world, a host of pixies who help Harry out from time to time in exchange for pizza, and a real live fairy godmother. But the cases just as often require him to work with the Chicago Police Department, giving a nice grounding for those less given to flights of fancy.

READING PATHS

If you like scruffy PIs that are smart (and smart mouthed) and want a mystery:

Monkey's Raincoat by Robert Crais

If you like to look at the magic that lives alongside the normal world and want a fantasy:

The Onion Girl by Charles de Lint

The City and the City by China Miéville

A great example of what can be wrought when you take a traditional genre structure but untether it from our mundane workaday world is this groundbreaking work of China Miéville. In *The City and the City*, we have all the hallmarks of a classic police procedural: a cop is confronted with a dead body and must search for clues, fight battles of jurisdiction, and wrangle with his own bureaucracy to catch the killer. But the twist is the thoroughly mind-bending setting. Our cop, Tyador Borlú, works in the imaginary Eastern European city of Beszel, which shares geography with its rival city of Ul Qoma. And this doesn't mean they are near neighbors, but rather, they are completely intermingled, and the citizens of each pursue a rigid, inviolate policy of "un-seeing" the other city. The fantasy elements are subtle (more description will not help—this is a book that must be experienced) and could be seen as an intriguing exercise in existential possibilities. But for those mystery readers who are willing to explore the borders of reality, illusion, and perception, this could be a rewarding read.

READING PATHS

If you like a touch of the surreal and a vivid setting but want a mystery:

The Manual of Detection by Jedediah Berry

If you like the weird cityscape and want a fantasy:

Windup Girl by Paolo Bacigalupi

Midnight Riot by Ben Aaronovitch (RIVERS OF LONDON, BOOK 1)

The British police procedural is a well-loved institution (all those constables and inspectors!), and adding in a fantasy world hiding in plain sight is the premise for this interesting blended series. Aaronovitch's first book introduces Metropolitan Police Constable Peter Grant. He begins the series as a probationary constable and is working a routine scene when he has an unusual interaction with a witness. The unusual part is that the witness is a ghost, and Peter's abilities to speak with the dead bring him to the attention of England's last wizard, DCI Nightingale, also of the Metropolitan Police. The hapless Peter is taken on as an apprentice by Nightingale and gets an introduction to the various Powers operating in London as the two try to find a vicious killer who can change his face. The series is an interesting mix of light and dark, with lots of humor but high-stakes violence and danger as well. The fantasy elements are balanced perfectly, giving us a secret-world feel for the magic underpinning London, while never forgetting the mystery plot that keeps us reading.

READING PATHS

If you like the dry, British wit but just want a mystery:

Orchestrated Death by Cynthia Harrod-Eagles

If you like a London filled with hidden magic and want a fantasy:

A Madness of Angels by Kate Griffin

Mystery/Historical Fiction

One of the best ways to add interest to a plain vanilla mystery is to add an interesting frame. Geographical setting and time period are important aspects of what we mean by frame, but in reality frame is more than that. Those who read for frame want to be transported to that frame through words. It's not enough to say that a book is set in a certain time; we need to have the details right to scratch the historical fiction itch. The clothes, the food, the very smell of the streets are all key to giving readers an immersive and satisfying historical fiction experience, and these can be folded into a mystery with great success. For mysteries, the historical frame also usually adds a crucial level of handicapping for the fictional detective. Crime solvers in modern times have many tools at their fingertips. From the CSI-type science of evidence examination and DNA analysis to the mundane realities of cell phones and GPS, today's detectives have an arsenal they can bring to bear to solve crimes. In other historical periods, investigators are hobbled by their levels of technology and sometimes by the strictures of society. When looking at the formula, these limitations all work to make interesting impediments, a crucial aspect of the plot arc. Just as with historical fiction in general, readers of historical mysteries are often drawn to particular settings—ancient Rome, WWI, turn-of-the-century New York, and so on. Luckily, the field is so thickly populated that you can almost always find an appealing pick, and it is not difficult to bridge the historical setting preferences, as long as your reader is not wedded to reading about a contemporary setting. The blends here may show how much crime investigation has changed but also reveal how little humanity's criminal urges have not.

A Test of Wills by Charles Todd (INSPECTOR RUTLEDGE, BOOK 1)

This series by Charles Todd succeeds quite well on both the mystery and history fronts. On the one hand you have a great historical frame:

shell-shocked Ian Rutledge has returned from the battlefields of WWI plagued by memories and ghosts. But the hook for mystery fans is that Rutledge is trying to pick up his work as an inspector with Scotland Yard. This first book shows Rutledge's first case since returning to the Yard; it's a political hot potato with a dead war hero and a suspect who is a close friend to royalty. The wounds of war are everywhere in this story. Author Todd (a mother-son writing team) gives us lots of details about what British life was like in those traumatic post-war years and has researched the period well. The hints we get of the huge psychological toll that war took on its participants make Rutledge more fully realized and flawed, a character readers will happily return to again and again. But, in addition to exploring the post-war scenery in each volume, Todd presents a carefully plotted, morally challenging crime story.

READING PATHS

If you like the exploration of the difficult path of those adjusting to life after WWI and want a mystery:

Maisie Dobbs by Jacqueline Winspear

If you like the look at the devastation of the WWI period and want historical fiction:

Regeneration by Pat Barker

Dissolution by C. J. Sansom (MATTHEW SHARDLAKE, BOOK 1)

In Sansom's Tudor-set mysteries featuring lawyer Matthew Shardlake, we get a vivid portrait of England on the cusp of huge change. Matthew is a hunchbacked lawyer in the service of Henry VIII's chief minister Thomas Cromwell who gets sent to handle difficult situations. In the first volume he is sent to investigate a murder at a Catholic monastery under consideration for dissolution by the crown. The investigations in this series tend to be morally snarled, dark, and thoroughly compelling. The characters are complex, the setting interesting, and the period details plentiful enough for any historical fiction fan. Few periods of history are as rife with game-changing pivot points, and Sansom shows us the politics, religion, and class conflict of the time through characters highborn and low. A common technique used in historical fiction is to view history through the lens of a "common man" close to the greater figures, and Sansom uses Shardlake skillfully in that manner: he can take us to manor houses and taverns with equal ease.

READING PATHS

If you like the Tudor setting and want a mystery:

To Shield the Queen by Fiona Buckley

If you like the look at the reign of Henry VIII and want historical fiction:

Autobiography of Henry VIII by Margaret George

The Sweetness at the Bottom of the Pie by Alan Bradley
(FLAVIA DE LUCE, BOOK 1)

Flavia de Luce lives in the decaying but genteel comfort of her family's English estate in 1950 in this first entry of a series. Highly precocious at the age of 11, Flavia possesses a scientific curiosity that embroils her in a murder investigation when a dead body turns up in the garden. Her father comes under suspicion, and Flavia must use all of her considerable wits and natural nosiness to find the real killer. The cozy setting and wry British sensibilities are charming, as is the unique heroine, despite her dramatic ways. Bradley artfully sprinkles the details of life at the estate and the nearby village that are the tools of good historical fiction. Post-war rationing tells in the details of clothing and food and the decline of formerly wealthy families and estates all root this story in its setting. This belongs to the classic school of British mysteries, with eccentric characters, red herrings, and a juicy evil villain. It's not a complicated puzzle and has a lightness that historical mysteries often do not, but the characters and setting paint a vivid picture of a time and place.

READING PATHS

If you like the cozy plot and eccentric cast and want a mystery:

Agatha Raisin and the Quiche of Death by M. C. Beaton

If you like small English village novels and want historical fiction:

A Month in the Country by J. L. Carr

Mystery/Horror

At a glance, mystery and horror might seem like they have a lot in common. They are both more likely than any other genre to have dead bodies littering their pages. But horror is a genre that doesn't always play well with others. Because of the emotional and visceral extremes that epitomize some of the core texts of the genre, it seems like a less than natural fit with other kinds of fiction. However, the mood and the atmosphere that are so crucial to horror can be found in mysteries, even if the monsters in the dark are usually of the human variety. To find mysteries that will also appeal to horror fans, look for the darker, gritty books. Ghosts (a horror staple) can pop up in a whole range of mysteries, even cozies where they tend to be of the helpful variety (Carolyn Hart's Bailey Ruth books are an example). Adding the darkness of a horror novel to a mystery can boost the suspense, as the writers of horror have a lock on the ability to make you dread what's coming. It can also give a palpable sense of evil to a plot, making the stakes seem higher and the outcome more uncertain. The borderlands where horror crosses over into urban fantasy can be tricky to navigate for librarians, although not as much for readers. As will be discussed in the fantasy and horror chapters, the different appeal can be how "other" the monster remains. But, if books still have a dark tone, a menacing atmosphere, and a real danger, then the traditional horror monsters can be incorporated into a blend with mysteries and break a few of those horror rules.

Black House by Stephen King and Peter Straub (Jack Sawyer, book 2)

Two masters of horror team up a second time for a supernatural mystery featuring retired homicide detective Jack Sawyer, who was the child protagonist of their first collaboration, *The Talisman*. In this sequel, taking place more than 20 years later, we get a story grounded in the horrors of our own world while still exploring the dimension known as the Territories. As the story begins, Jack has no memory of the Territories, although the threat of those memories returning was a reason he left the police force. When a series of horrific killings are committed in a small Wisconsin town, the local chief of police asks Jack to help with the investigation. But his involvement causes him to start having disturbing waking dreams that will eventually lead him back to the Territories and the horrors of his past. The crime and horror elements are skillfully melded, as are the styles of the two authors, with Straub's elegant writing and King's powerful visual images working together seamlessly. There are also rewards here for fans of King's Dark Tower series with many allusions to that universe, although there is no real barrier to new fans engaging with this work. The vivid characters and emotionally charged story make the narrative even more powerful as you worry as much for Jack and his companions as you do about the fate of the world.

READING PATHS

If you like suppressed memories but want a more straightforward mystery:

Bones to Ashes by Kathy Reichs

If you like plots with other dimensions and want more horror:

The Doorkeepers by Graham Masterton

Guilty Pleasures by Laurell K. Hamilton (ANITA BLAKE, BOOK 1)

The Anita Blake series has undergone a lot of changes over more than 20 books, from a mystery-centered world where the monsters are "other" and dangerous in the first books to a more fantasy-based series that keeps the dark tone but pairs it with erotic sensuality and immersion into the world of the monster. Both early and late books have their fans, but I would say that they are almost two different series and could be handled as such in a readers' advisory situation. *Guilty Pleasures*, the first volume of the series, has Anita hired to find out who is killing St. Louis's newly legal vampire citizens. The world building in this first volume is solid, imagining a society in which the monsters under the bed have come out and want to assimilate under the protection of the law. But these monsters are dangerous, and Hamilton adds a dark tone and menace to her monsters that will appeal to a horror fan. Anita's job is to hunt down the vampires when they step outside the law, but she is also a powerful necromancer—raiser of the dead—in her own right. The dichotomy of good monsters and bad monsters is set from this first volume and runs through the series, although the focus of the series takes a turn away from the mysteries and toward the relationships around book nine. For fans of the early books, Anita Blake is a model for many of the tough, determined urban-fantasy heroines who came after.

READING PATHS

If you like heroines with angsty, sexy, monster-filled love lives that still have a mystery:

Dead Witch Walking by Kim Harrison

If you don't mind a sympathetic monster and want more horror:

The Last Werewolf by Glen Duncan

Already Dead **by Charlie Huston (Joe Pitt, book 1)**

New York City is chock-full of vampires, all intent on defending their turf while staying off the radar of the oblivious human population. Joe Pitt might be a blood sucker, but he doesn't particularly want to join any of the powers that be, preferring to remain an independent operator, answerable to no one. Still, there are bills to pay and blood supplies to secure, so he agrees to find a rich runaway, which brings him back into contact with the powerful Coalition. They also want him to track down the source of a weird bacterium that is on the loose and causing some conspicuous zombie-like behavior. Can't have that if you want to keep the undead a secret. The nonstop violence done by and to our antihero is not for the faint of heart, but for a new and entertaining look at the seedy underbelly of vampiric Manhattan, this series is hard to beat. Pitt's antiauthority attitude and penchant for finding the most difficult way through any problem will remind readers of PIs from the noir canon.

READING PATHS

If you like a hero who always follows a personal code and want a mystery:

The Godwulf Manuscript by Robert B. Parker

If you like vampires with a noirish edge and want horror:

Bloodlist by P. N. Elrod

Mystery/Romance

Even though many, many mystery fans are women, the genre as a whole is one of the more reliably male-friendly out there. This does not have to change when you add a romance. After all, if there is one genre that is most consistently crossed with others, it is romance. The reasons for this are not hard to understand: romantic relationships are a real or aspirational part of almost every life, and adding romance to a story line humanizes characters. Does your mystery have a curmudgeonly misanthropic character who needs more appeal? Give him a girlfriend. As much as a romantic relationship is a normal thing, it is also a great fulcrum for drama. Have a story that needs a spark? Put the protagonist's loved one in danger. Every story needs conflict, and the conflict that a romantic arc can bring is often a writer's go-to tool for moving a story along. For whatever reason an author decides to inject romance into a mystery, the addition can definitely change the appeal. Adding an emotional genre to an intellectual one like mystery means that you can draw in people who normally think mysteries are too dry, too analytical, too—dare I say it?—masculine. This does not mean that blending in romance automatically turns a hard-boiled mystery into chick lit. How the romance is framed and its centrality to the story usually helps a readers' advisor know whether a mystery/romance blend will work for a traditional mystery fan. These blends are commonly found at the cozy end of the mystery spectrum, where the violence quotient is lower and the pace slower, leaving plenty of time for romantic developments. This is also where you usually find the husband-wife teams such as the leads of Carolyn Hart's Death on Demand series or Max and Sarah from Charlotte MacLeod's Boston-set cozies. While the romantic tension might not be as exciting for these longer-standing couples, the push and pull of a real relationship can add depth to the characterization in a mystery. In this chapter, where the focus is on mystery genre fans, I chose titles that evidence all the traditional mystery appeal factors but add romance. In the romance chapter, I will discuss titles that are firmly in the romance camp.

In the Bleak Midwinter by Julia Spencer-Fleming
(CLAIRE FERGUSSON, BOOK 1)

This first book in a series showcases the fascinating relationship between Russ Van Alstyne, police chief in the small upstate New York town of Millers Kill, and Claire Fergusson, an ex-Army pilot and current Episcopalian priest. Claire has just moved to town to take over the local parish, and a foundling baby is left at her church. While working together to find the baby's mother, Claire and Russ soon expose a murder that will unravel secrets and reveal personal demons. The attraction and chemistry between the two will appeal to romance fans willing to forgo the immediate happy ending. The complications and impediments to their relationship (including a very large one: Russ is already married at the beginning of the series) mean that it progresses at a slow burn, but one that keeps you reading on in the series hoping for their happiness. In this first book, as in later entries, the focus is on characters but not at the expense of story. The series also shows how small towns can complicate criminal investigations, as the investigators are often embedded in the community in a different way than cops in a big city. The mystery here is deftly plotted, with good tension sustained throughout and a gripping climax. But the characters are what readers will want to return to, volume after volume, rooting for their happy endings.

READING PATHS

If you like the combo of violent crimes with up-and-down romantic relationship plots developed over multiple books and want a mystery:

A Share in Death by Deborah Crombie

If you like the darkness at the heart of a community and want suspense with more romance:

Heartbreaker by Julie Garwood

One for the Money by Janet Evanovich (STEPHANIE PLUM, BOOK 1)

Amateur sleuths are usually much luckier in the love department than their professional counterparts, but Janet Evanovich's bail enforcement heroine, Stephanie Plum, has managed to keep her love life well tangled over the course of a series that is into the double digits. In her first outing, Stephanie is out of work and decides to try her hand at her cousin's bail enforcement office. However, being a bounty hunter is harder than it looks when one of her first assignments is to bring in Joe Morelli, a former vice cop and the rat who took Stephanie's virginity when she was 16. This series has a truly wacky cast of supporting characters, lots of humor, and great sexual attraction between not only Stephanie and Morelli, but also Stephanie and her bounty hunting sensei, Ranger. The man-balancing act that author Evanovich sustains over the series means that this is not a slam dunk for romance fans looking for a definitive happily-ever-after ending, but the palpable chemistry and snappy, flirty dialogue will have a familiar appeal for readers of many romances. From Evanovich a reader could easily move back and forth between the lighter amateur mysteries and contemporary romances.

READING PATHS

If you like sassy heroines and want a light, humorous mystery:

The Spellman Files by Lisa Lutz

If you like spunky leading ladies and big doses of humor and want a romance:

Bet Me by Jennifer Crusie

Naked in Death by J. D. Robb (In Death, book 1)

A romantic couple together for dozens of books might seem like boring stuff, but J. D. Robb's Eve and Roarke are still a smoking-hot couple whose relationship gains depth and adds dimension to each new volume of this police procedural series. The series is unusual as it is a successful blend of not just two major genres (mystery and romance), but it adds a third with its SF-influenced near-future setting. The SF elements need not scare off those who avoid that genre, however, as they mostly consist of some futuristic set dressing and a few cool toys. The heart of the series has always been both the tightly plotted, gritty mysteries and the sexy devotion of the lead couple. In this series opener, Eve Dallas is a police lieutenant in mid-21st-century New York who keeps the world at bay through a passionate devotion to her job. A horrific childhood on the streets gave her a traumatic start to life but also made her into a strong if guarded seeker of justice. When she is assigned a case involving a dead prostitute, the main suspect is billionaire industrialist Roarke, and the two spend some quality time fighting their attraction while Eve searches for the real killer.

READING PATHS

If you like a guarded, damaged heroine and want a mystery:

Shakespeare's Landlord by Charlaine Harris

If you like suspenseful plots and strong women and want more romance:

Mr. Perfect by Linda Howard

Mystery/Science Fiction

The readers of science fiction have one thing in common with the readers of mysteries: they are both statistically and historically likely to be of the analytical persuasion. They like books that involve puzzles, whether of the whodunit variety found in mysteries or the more esoteric "what would that be like?" questions that live at the heart of SF. This, however, does not mean that all mystery fans like SF or vice versa. Again, it can come down to a willingness to step outside of one's own world. Expanding one's idea of what is possible can open up a reader to the worlds of SF. Both are categorized by Joyce Saricks as genres that appeal to the intellect (Saricks 2009) and that make for interesting opportunities to find books that appeal to both sets of fans. The wide spectrum of possible questions explored in SF can range from a near-future glimpse of where our current path of science and technology is taking us to a far-flung space-faring culture and the questions of how we might interact with another sentient species. Finding where along that spectrum of "what if?" a reader is in the mood for is key to finding a blend that will work for him. As we see with fantasy, frame is also an important part of what science fiction can bring to the party in a genre blend. The cool gadgets and advanced technologies are a big part of why readers enjoy SF, and these window-dressing elements can be added to a mystery without troubling the core fan base. When the focus shifts to the big picture of what society would be like in a changed "what if?" world, then we usually have moved more firmly into the SF camp, and those blends will be considered in the science fiction chapter. When SF is done well, it is a new lens through which to view humanity, including the sad truth of the crimes we commit upon one another. Adding SF to a mystery lets the author use that new "what if?" lens—of alien cultures, technological advancement, galactic exploration—and see how we still must face our human demons.

The Yiddish Policemen's Union by Michael Chabon

The fact that this book won both the Hugo and the Nebula awards (the two best-known SF awards) and was also shortlisted for the Edgar (the premier mystery award) should tell you a little about how well this book works for both fan bases. Chabon has long dabbled with genre fiction, and this novel falls into the subcategory of science fiction that deals with alternative history. This branch is concerned with the "what if?" questions of the past. How would our world be different if a pivotal point in history had a different outcome? The divergent point in Chabon's new world is during WWII. He posits a scenario in which the Jews of Europe were offered a homeland in Alaska, not Israel, and from that small premise we get a vivid portrait of a possible world. This world is just as crime filled as our own, sadly, requiring police detectives like our hero Meyer Landsman, who is a depressed, alcoholic noir archetype but with soul. When a man is murdered in his rooming house, Landsman investigates and becomes embroiled in plots and schemes and politics that are far over his head. The culture clash between the Jews of Sitka and the Native Americans they displaced is just one of the many interesting SF possibilities explored in Chabon's alternate history, and they all add to what would have been a solid character-driven detective story on its own. This is a great example of how two genres can come together and the resulting story elevates both genres to new creative levels.

READING PATHS

If you like the noir tradition of troubled men in over their heads and want a mystery:

The Big Sleep by Raymond Chandler

If you like alternative history using WWII as a pivot point and want something SF:

Farthing by Jo Walton

When Gravity Fails by George Alec Effinger (Marîd Audran, book 1)

The 1980s saw the birth of a new subgenre of SF dubbed cyberpunk, stemming from the rapid changes in technology and heavily influenced by the darker, gritty end of the crime fiction shelves. Although the SF/thriller *Neuromancer* by William Gibson was the poster child for the category, George Alec Effinger's *When Gravity Fails* is another early example and actually seems more possible and less dated than many cyberpunk novels. It is a future with mobile phones and designer drugs, where people can choose to have ports into their brains that allow for personality "moddies" to be popped in and out. Set in an unnamed Islamic city in Northern Africa, this first book in a trilogy follows Marid Audran through the back alleys of the seedy red light district, the Budayeen. He is a drug addict and a freelance detective of sorts, balanced between the corrupt cops and the more corrupt crime kingpins, associating almost exclusively with prostitutes and hustlers. The writing is spare but fantastic, vividly calling up a unique futuristic setting, and filled with the rhythms of the Arab world and the wry voice of its flawed protagonist.

READING PATHS

If you like the setting in the Arab world and want a mystery:

Finding Nouf by Zoë Ferraris

If you like the cyberpunk with an exotic setting and want more SF:

Pashazade by Jon Courtenay Grimwood

The Last Policeman by Ben H. Winters (HANK PALACE, BOOK 1)

How would you behave if you knew the world was going to end? That is the science fiction question behind this mystery novel. A planet-killing asteroid is heading for Earth, and while some folks have checked out early by suicide, most others have simply walked off their jobs and decided to sit out the end. Hank Palace has finally achieved his life's desire to be a detective in the Concord police department due to staff attrition, and he has no intention of leaving his post. When Peter Zell is found dead in a fast-food restaurant bathroom, his death is ruled a suicide, but Hank thinks there is more to it. With authentic dialogue and an intriguing look at a doggedly determined cop trying to keep everything by the book despite the fact that the world is about to end, author Winters balances the two genres perfectly. The breakdown of societal norms and expectations is fascinating with all the dark and violent aspects of human nature on display when people feel like they have nothing to lose. Everyone around Hank wants him to let this case slide, to not care so much. While there is humor in Hank's efforts to live up to his new detective shield under the circumstances, he is a character that will fight to honor the proper procedures of police work, even as he has to brush up on them himself.

READING PATHS

If you like the difficult circumstances and settings that challenge the detective but want a mystery:

Skull Mantra by Eliot Pattison

If you like a look at with how people face the impending end of the world and want more SF:

Flood by Stephen Baxter

WORKING WITH MYSTERY BLENDS

The variety of ways that authors have managed to use the simple but satisfying ingredients of a mystery in the blends above shows both the power of the formula and its flexibility. Knowing when to suggest one of these books or one of the dozens of others that mixes mystery with another genre is all about knowing what kind of read your patrons are looking for in that moment. Do they want a playful homage to the conventions of mystery? Are they looking for a new genre experience that borrows the structure of a classic mystery? Or have they never read a mystery before but want to ease into the experience by way of another, more familiar genre? There are blends for all of these readers. Whether a reader is a lifelong lover of mysteries looking for a new twist on a favorite genre, or even if he thinks he doesn't like mysteries at all, the answer could be to try a blend.

6

ROMANCE BLENDS
Blends That Are Looking for True Love

Romance as a genre is a huge part of the publishing landscape as a whole, and it outsells every other genre according to statistics compiled annually by the Romance Writers of America. Why so much love for books about love? One big reason is that almost all of us from puberty onward want our own love story. The usual ingredients in any romance are two people who feel an attraction for each other. The couple is most often a man and a woman, but there is also a small but robust segment of the romance market aimed at same-sex romance. For simplicity's sake, I might refer to the couple throughout this chapter with terms like the "hero" and "heroine," but boy meets girl could also mean boy meets boy or girl meets girl. The boom in e-books has benefitted romance more than any other genre and has increased not only the number of romances on the market, but also their diversity. This means that it is easier than ever for romance fans to find their lives reflected in the books they read. In the typical romance, the main couple is introduced fairly early on, often in an awkward but endearing fashion, known in the genre as the "meet cute." A variation on the meet cute is to have the couple meet in some heightened situation so that they are immediately in conflict. But whether it is a case of love at first sight or hate at first sight, the initial meeting is about attraction and sparks. Once a couple is brought together, an author must find a reason to keep the pair apart. If they meet and there is no conflict, it would be a pretty short book. Instant happy ending. That is not nearly as satisfying as a couple that goes through obstacles to get to their happy ending. Conflict and obstacles give a romance its shape and its plot.

The romance genre may have the universal core plot of a love story, but it also contains a lot of variety. Because there are a lot of ways to tell a love story, romance contains dozens of subgenres that appeal to different audiences. General romance or contemporary romance is usually a story set in the present day where the couple meet and have to contend with the kind of obstacles any regular reader might identify with: family, jobs, misunderstandings, and miscommunications. The arc of the story usually involves bringing the couple together, pulling them apart, and then bringing them back together again. There can be several cycles of this presentation of and overcoming of obstacles. Traditionally in romances it doesn't matter how much conflict comes in the middle; the end must have the couple together. This end piece, the happily ever after, is essential to most romance readers. The variations in the way this story arc is presented are often brought about by blending in other genres, but if the main focus and narrative energy of a book remain on bringing about the couple's happy ending, it is still a romance. Conversely, there can be many books in the general fiction stacks or in other genres that include some aspects of a love story, but unless the reader gets to spend time with the main couple and gets the emotionally satisfying happy ending—the book can be romantic as all get out—it is not a romance.

APPEAL OF ROMANCE

Characters are at the heart of the appeal for romance. Because at its most basic level a romance is a simple story of boy meets girl, you have to care about those two characters. While some genres can have unlikeable characters or unreliable narrators, romance works best when you root for the couple. That doesn't mean that your heroine has to be all sunshine and light or your hero a one-note paragon. Character growth is often a very important part of a romance. This growth can be the conflict that forms the plot when one or both love interests have to adjust their lives or their thinking to be with each other. Because most romance readers are women, the heroine of a romance is especially important. No other genre has the story consistently revolve around a woman. She usually has the power in a romance story, being the character with the agency (whether or not she uses it) to choose or reject the hero and to improve her own life because of her choices. The heroine is often the primary point-of-view character and will be the reader's main doorway to the story. Romance heroines are usually smart, strong, and interesting because the reader will be spending time in her head. The hero can be dark and mysterious, even a little dangerous. This will make the eventual surrender of that hero to the love story even more dramatic.

Emotional engagement in the story is what most romance readers are looking for in the genre. This can be established through language and plot, but it is easiest to engage a reader's emotions through character. Chemistry is key because it doesn't matter how well written two characters are if you don't feel their attraction on the page. The skillful romance writer can make a reader actually feel the butterflies of attraction, flush with the heat of sensuality, and long desperately for a happy resolution. The fact that a writer can evoke an emotional response with mere words is one of the most amazing things about literature in general, and romance in particular. There are other appeals to romance besides a likeable central couple, however. Well-drawn secondary characters can add a lot to a story, both as support for the hero and heroine or as antagonists or points of conflict. Setting can also be a huge appeal, with vivid pictures of small-town life, urban drama, or exotic locales. Finally, the plot, with the search for and attainment of true love, is of course a huge draw. The desire for romantic love in our own lives is an almost universal human characteristic. Romance can, of course, be a wish-fulfillment genre, through which readers vicariously achieve a perfect happy love-story ending that is rarely attainable in real life. But it should not be derided (and often is) as mere escapism or fantasy. Romances are a unique genre in literature not only because they focus on examining relationships and emotions, but also because of the centrality they place on women's lives and experiences.

WHY BLEND?

Love stories can be found in every genre. In other chapters, I have tried mostly to highlight books that may have strong romance story lines, but those romances share plot space with another genre and are not necessarily the focus of the overall story. In this chapter, the romance is the heart of the story, with the other genres providing settings, frames, and conflict for the central love story. As mentioned above, there are a lot of romance readers out there. However, many people feel self-conscious about reading romance books, and that is at least in part due to the way they are marketed. A cruise through the romance aisles of any bookstore shows lots of bare-chested men and women falling out of pretty dresses. E-books have helped a lot of romance readers be less self-conscious about the books they read, as the anonymous container of an e-reading device means no one has to know your book cover has a half-naked Scotsman on the cover. Blending some other genres with romance can change how they are marketed. For example, when you add a mystery or adrenaline, the book will usually be marketed as romantic suspense rather than romance, and its cover will be much more subdued. Other genres like historical fiction, science fiction, and fantasy are likely to be marketed squarely at the romance crowd when they are in a blend, with covers to indicate they are romance forward. This might be one case in which the publishers know that the reading public has a huge appetite for love stories and markets accordingly. Romance is one genre in which blends have been happening for a long time, and each genre that gets added to romance can end up as a popular subgenre under the romance umbrella.

THE BLENDS

Romance/Adrenaline

Adding danger, action, and suspense to a romance results in the subgenre of romantic suspense. This large subgenre is still mostly read by women, but it does pull readers from both the adrenaline and romance aisles. There is wide variety in the titles that get marketed as romantic suspense, from titles where the focus is on the adrenaline plot and the romance is a complication to those where the adrenaline aspects are the obstacle to the love story. Romantic suspense can be edgy, violent, and sexually explicit; or it can be none of those things. This range in tone makes it important to talk with romantic suspense fans about what kind of reading experience they are seeking. Most romantic suspense books keep a fair amount of the narrative energy about the central couple. They must spend time together responding to each other and not just reacting to the dangerous plot to be a good bet for romance fans. People thrown together in a crisis where emotions are heightened and their lives are in danger might find it easy to mistake that adrenaline rush for love, so it is up to the author to give that romantic relationship depth and to show why the hero and heroine are meant to be. A lot of romantic suspense story lines involve strong, professional alpha males coming to the rescue of women in trouble. This can be very satisfying for readers, but there needs to be a connection made beyond a simple rescue. The heroine has to have some agency of her own and should participate in the action. For most romantic suspense (and certainly for titles that appeal to traditional romance fans), readers have to believe that the couple have a future, a happily ever after, even after the danger is past.

Cry No More by **Linda Howard**

Linda Howard is a prolific writer in the romance genre, but many of her novels also have a high quotient of suspense. *Cry No More* has enough action to satisfy a thriller reader of any gender, but it is also a novel crafted to deeply appeal to women. Milla Edge was living in Mexico when her six-week-old baby was stolen from her in the marketplace, vanished without a trace. The loss devastated her, destroyed her marriage, and set her on a path to make sure the same thing didn't happen to other women. Milla devotes her life to an organization she founded to help find missing people, especially children, but she never gives up on finding her son. When the cold trail gets hot again, she teams up with a man known on both sides of the border as Diaz. Diaz has the cold eyes of a killer, but he also has contacts that Milla needs in her search. From El Paso to Juarez and points beyond, the two work together until Milla finds that her fear of Diaz is gone and she only feels attraction. Skillfully playing on the fear that will haunt any mother, the author builds the tension as Milla finally gets closer than ever to her son, but also gets closer to some very dangerous people. Diaz is a strong, silent alpha male (common in both the adrenaline and romance genres), and there is nothing sexier than an alpha male who falls hard. When romantic suspense is done well it can put the reader through an emotional wringer, and Howard knows just how to turn the crank.

READING PATHS

If you like the missing children advocate and want a romance:

Mine to Possess by Nalini Singh

If you like the danger at the Mexico border and want a thriller:

Iron River by T. Jefferson Parker

Unsung Hero by **Suzanne Brockmann** (Troubleshooters, book 1)

This is the first in a series of romances featuring Navy SEALs, full of gripping action and compelling romance. When *Unsung Hero* begins, the setup seems like a classic contemporary romance: two people who had the hots for each other when they were teens are drawn back together, with sparks ensuing. Tom Paoletti is a Navy SEAL who has returned to his small New England hometown to convalesce from a terrible head injury. Kelly Ashton is a successful pediatrician home to take care of her dying father. The two were attracted when they were younger, but nothing came of it. Now they are thrown together again and the heat is still there, but can they fit into each other's lives as adults? The adrenaline starts creeping into the story slowly, with Tom sure he has seen a famous terrorist in town, but afraid he's hallucinating from his injury. He calls in his SEAL buddies, but while he's waiting for them he and Kelly get to know each other again. The action picks up in the last third of the book, as it looks like Tom was right and this terrorist is in town to set off a bomb during an anniversary celebration of a local WWII regiment. The romance between Tom and Kelly has its ups and downs, but the chemistry and friendship between the two are both hot and sweet.

READING PATHS

If you like the mix of Navy SEAL hero and want an even sexier romance:

Wild Card by Lora Leigh

If you like the Navy SEAL action and want a thriller:

Executive Power by Vince Flynn

Something About You **by Julie James (FBI/US Attorney, book 1)**

Although hardcover romantic suspense is what makes up the bulk of the romance/adrenaline blends that are published, there are some books marketed straight at the romance audience that also contain action and thrills. Attorney Cameron Lynde is staying at a hotel where a prostitute has been killed in the next room. The FBI, led by Special Agent Jack Pallas, is involved because it looks like the prostitute's client was a high ranking US senator. Jack and Cameron have a history, but they're going to have to set aside their differences to solve the case before the killers realize Cameron was a witness and come after her. *Something About You* actually benefits from having the shorter format of a paperback original romance, as it does away with some of the unnecessary complications typical of romantic suspense. Cameron doesn't pretend she can take care of herself; when she realizes her danger, she asks for help. The two leads talk through their conflict rather than have it drag out for chapters. There are still some great angry sparks that turn into sexy sparks, but it doesn't take a hundred pages to get there, and the tone is lightened by a lot of humor and an interesting supporting cast. The action complements and is a catalyst for the romance without overpowering the story, which would make this a good entry for those interested in trying out a low-key example of romantic suspense.

READING PATHS

If you like the sexy FBI hero and want a romance:

Betrayal by Danielle Steel

If you like plot of a female witness who becomes a target and want a thriller:

Saving Faith by David Baldacci

Romance/Fantasy

Another blend that is popular enough to be an established subgenre with hundreds of books published every year is the romance/fantasy. These blends are marketed and identified by readers under the category called paranormal romance. While there are other ways to combine the two genres with the focus on building an elaborate secondary fantasy world, those titles are less likely to be marketed to romance readers. The blends that end up on the romance shelves are usually based on a real-world setting that happens to contain magic, making them sexier cousins to urban fantasy. Paranormal romance is where the alpha males really tend to come out and play. While many romances feature a strong, dominant hero who surrenders to his need for the heroine, this theme is writ large when the hero is a centuries-old magical creature or an actual alpha wolf. While most romances have a strong heroine (or at least a heroine who comes to find her strength during the story), this is especially true in paranormal romances, where the kick-butt heroine is a mainstay and the struggle becomes how to balance her supernatural nature or responsibilities with a desire for love.

Halfway to the Grave by Jeaniene Frost (Night Huntress, book 1)

Cat Crawfield is something that was thought impossible: half human, half vampire. Cat spent her teen years seeking out vampires and using her half-breed speed and strength to kill them, and has racked up quite a body count, but she finally picks a victim who is not going down so easily. When Cat targets vampire Bones in a bar and tries to lure him to his death, he quickly turns the tables on her, but rather than killing her he convinces her they should work together. He also kills vampires (for money), and Cat is the ideal bait for hungry vamps: lovely and vulnerable and human in appearance, but deadly. As Bones trains Cat, an attraction grows between the two, and soon they're sleeping together as well as hunting together. The romance works because Cat must fight her lifelong hatred of vampires to be with Bones, and of course overcome a hefty dose of self-hatred too. Bones is a delicious hero: gorgeous, British, and a dead-ringer for Spike from *Buffy the Vampire Slayer*. Exchanges between Cat and Bones are funny and sexy, and this first book will leave readers wanting to read the rest of the series to continue their story. This is a classic example of the horror monster of the vampire being subverted into more of a standard fantasy villain rather than the implacable evil of horror. There are still scary vampires out there, but Frost has stripped out the pacing and tension of horror for fantasy (and romance) attributes instead.

READING PATHS

If you like the vampire hunters but want more romance:

Dark Lover by J. R. Ward

If you like the vampire hunter but want more fantasy:

Dhampir by Barb Hendee and J. C. Hendee

Firelight by Kristen Callihan (DARKEST LONDON, BOOK 1)

Even though historical settings are an enormous part of the romance genre, there are fewer paranormal romances set in the past. This merging of two of the most popular subgenres works extremely well in *Firelight*. In Victorian England Miranda Ellis has been forced to wed to save her family from financial ruin. Her bridegroom is the notorious aristocrat Benjamin Archer, who has a terrible reputation and hides his face behind a mask. Both Miranda and Archer enter the arrangement with enormous secrets, so it surprises both that their marriage of convenience might also include a passionate attraction. When Archer is accused of murder soon after the wedding, the two must learn to work together and trust each other to clear his name. Only the abilities that Miranda has kept secret for so long will save Archer from the curse he has been living under, and the stakes are high when the two realize they love each other. Those who enjoy emotionally intense paranormal romances with tormented heroes who are redeemed by love should enjoy this unique historical twist on the theme.

READING PATHS

If you like the marriage of convenience that turns to love and want romance:

The Bargain by Mary Jo Putney

If you like the cursed hero saved by love and want a fantasy:

Beauty by Robin McKinley

Slave to Sensation by Nalini Singh (Psy/Changeling, book 1)

Nalini Singh gives her paranormal romance series an interesting complexity by populating a through-the-looking-glass version of our world with three main races: regular plain-vanilla humans; Changelings, who can shift between human and any animal species; and the Psy, the psychically gifted but emotionally cold race that dominates the political and business spheres. The three groups don't usually have much contact, but Psy Sascha Duncan meets Lucas, the alpha of the DarkRiver pack of Changeling leopards, when the two groups decide to go in together on a business deal. Sascha is a cardinal Psy, one of immense potential, but she must constantly build up her psychic shields so that people don't realize she is "flawed" due to her ability to feel emotions. Lucas senses that Sascha is different from the rest of the Psy, and that—as well as the immediate attraction he feels for her—convinces him to trust her with the knowledge that his people believe a Psy serial killer is murdering Changeling women. Sascha and Lucas make for a compelling study in opposites attracting, but they have huge obstacles in their path, including the traditional hatred of Changeling for the Psy and Sascha having to overcome years of conditioning that tell her that to feel any emotion is to be broken. The struggles of Sascha to open herself up to touch and warmth and love is especially heartrending as only she can find the Psy who is killing Lucas's people, and she doesn't think she will survive. Both the Changeling and Psy societies are fascinating, and future volumes in the series promise to explore this world further.

READING PATHS

If you like the heroine who has to learn to feel emotions and want a romance:

No Rest for the Wicked by Kresley Cole

If you like the different supernatural races working together and want a fantasy:

Cast in Shadow by Michelle Sagara

Romance/Historical

Historicals have always been a big part of the romance genre, with time periods ranging from prehistory through more recent times (although there are some eras that attract writers like catnip, such as the early 19th-century English Regency period or the American frontier). No matter the period chosen for a romance, that time will influence how the story unfolds and how the characters behave. A historical setting can be the source of the conflict in a plot, such as when the rules or expectations of society keep a couple apart. Historic events and situations such as war, disease, or the social mores of the day can provide more obstacles than any modern couple ever has to face, and those big hurdles add the drama that draws so many readers to historical romance. Some historical romances that are perfectly enjoyable could be termed "wallpaper historicals." What's usually meant by this is a book in which the author includes enough historical details to make the period identifiable, such as the clothes or the names of the rulers of the day, but there is not an abundance of history inserted beyond those surface details. The characters might have a more modern sensibility, the slang might not be period authentic, or the little details of daily life might not be fleshed out. This doesn't mean that readers won't still have a great time reading these kinds of historical romances, but they probably won't learn much about the time and place these books use as their settings. The trick to writing satisfying romances that convey an immersive historical reading experience seems to come down to research. There are many historical romances that read like the only research the author did was to read other historical romances. But if authors have done their research, they can add the little details that serve to ground a story in a period. Those could be small things like the kind of coach an aristocrat might ride in to big things like making sure a character behaves in accordance to the social rules of the day. Everybody likes a spunky heroine who's a rule breaker, but the author has to show that the character *knows* she is breaking the rules for it to have anything but a jarring anachronistic effect. As with any historical fiction writing, authors working in historical romances have to find a way to do enough research so they understand completely the lives and situations of their characters but then to leave most of that research out. The reader wants the story to be about the hero and the heroine, but having a detailed and convincing frame is a great way to add interest and conflict to the story.

Into the Wilderness by Sara Donati (WILDERNESS, BOOK 1)

Elizabeth Middleton has come to join her father and brother living at the edge of the untamed wilderness of upstate New York in the year 1792. Her father is a local judge and has carved a fair amount of land holdings out of the countryside, but it is all at risk due to poor decisions and gambling debt. Elizabeth is the answer to the judge's problems, and he soon schemes to wed his daughter to a wealthy doctor in town. But Elizabeth has a mind of her own, and since the first moment she laid eyes on Nathaniel Bonner, she cannot think of anyone else. Nathaniel is the son of the judge's old friend Hawkeye (yes, from James Fenimore Cooper's *Last of the Mohicans*), a white man raised among the native tribes, and while his family needs the land that comes as Elizabeth's dowry, Nathaniel desperately wants Elizabeth for herself. The two lovers face more obstacles than would seem possible, including near death and constant separation, all the while working to secure not only their own happiness but also the safety of Nathaniel's native family. Mixing in classic literary characters serves to ground this story even more convincingly in its historical setting, and it's just plain fun to revisit Hawkeye and Chingachgook. Nathaniel and his native family face prejudice and hatred from the local townspeople, but Nathaniel and Elizabeth never stop fighting for their chance to be together. It's swooningly romantic, with two strong-willed people trying to find a way to bend enough to let themselves be happy.

READING PATHS

If you like the story involving lovers torn between white and native cultures and want a romance:

Comanche Woman by Joan Johnston

If you like the conflict between settlers and native peoples and want more historical fiction:

Dances with Wolves by Michael Blake

An Infamous Army by **Georgette Heyer**

Georgette Heyer wrote dozens of historical romances that remain some of the most beloved works in the genre, but she also had a longing to write more respected works of historical fiction. She successfully managed to combine the two with *An Infamous Army*, which retains the sparkling wit and romance she is known for but combines it with one of the most accurate depictions of the Battle of Waterloo ever put on the page. The action begins among a group of wealthy Brits living in Brussels. Army Captain Charles Audley is expected to marry a demure and proper English girl but instead proposes to the scandalous widow Lady Barbara Childe. Bab is a wild flirt and tries to scare Charles away with outrageous antics but is also warm, generous, and *deserving* of Charles, if only she can realize that fact. By the time Heyer gets to the battle of Waterloo, readers will be too invested in the characters and the story to mind a detailed recounting of the historic event, which, in fact, adds great tension to the love story. Because Heyer's way with words doesn't stop with pretty dresses and carriages, readers will get a great romance as well as a rich and vivid picture of a historical time and place.

READING PATHS

If you like the scandalous woman finding true love and want a romance:

A Matter of Class by Mary Balogh

If you like the details of the Battle of Waterloo and want historical fiction:

Sharpe's Waterloo by Bernard Cornwell

Silk Is for Seduction by **Loretta Chase** (Dressmakers, book 1)

Loretta Chase is often called out as the standard bearer for well-researched, authentic historicals, usually during or just after the Regency period. Although most historicals keep their milieu tightly focused on the aristocracy of the era, that doesn't really give a full picture of the time period. Chase helps fill this historical void here by having her heroine, Marcelline Noirot, be a humble dressmaker in 1830s London. Well, not so humble really, as Marcelline is determined to be the most famous dressmaker in London and needs a high-profile client to get there. She sets her sights on the fiancée of the Duke of Clevedon, but things don't go as planned when the Duke decides to seduce Marcelline. The romance of two strong-willed characters that have fabulous chemistry is fleshed out with great supporting characters, witty dialogue, and a sumptuously detailed frame including lovely descriptions of the fashions of the period.

READING PATHS

If you like the couple from different social strata and want a historical romance:

Secrets of a Summer Night by Lisa Kleypas

If you like the 1830s setting and want historical fiction:

The Dress Lodger by Sheri Holman

Romance/Horror

Although there is a long history of sensuality in horror, there isn't a lot of romance. Women in old-school horror are usually there to fall victim to the monster, adding drama and sometimes a not-so-subtle cautionary message about sex. You can still have a romance that involves a couple facing real horrors together, but those are hard to find. The modern trend toward nuanced monsters means that it is likely to find a romance/horror blend that has the formerly scary monsters of werewolves, vampires, and demons turned into love interests. To be fair, romance has always liked the bad-boy heroes. Dark, tortured alpha male reformed by the love of a good woman is a story as old as romance itself. And it doesn't get more tortured than a vampire or more alpha than a werewolf. The trick is to find these kinds of blends that keep some of the darkness and some of the dread and danger of the horror genre. The high stakes and danger of horror can be used as a source of the conflict the central couple must cope with before they can be together, but the trick is to not have that conflict overpower the love story. A final compromise that has to happen when blending horror into a romance is that the reader needs to get more closure than horror usually likes to provide. If evil is eternal in most horror scenarios, romance blends usually soften that message. Love, after all, conquers all.

Bitten by Kelley Armstrong (WOMEN OF THE UNDERWORLD, BOOK 1)

Elena Michaels is trying to live a quiet life as a grad student in Toronto, blending in with the mundanes and hiding the fact that she is a werewolf—in fact the only known female werewolf. She is called by the alpha of her pack who wants her help in tracking a group of murderous "mutts" (werewolves unaffiliated with a pack), which forces Elena to deal with her animal nature. All of this is deeply complicated by the fact that Elena was changed into a werewolf by her fiancé, Clay, who hid his wolf from her and turned her without her consent. Denying both her own nature and her continued feelings for Clay is exhausting, and Elena will have to choose her path. The werewolf trope is a classic of horror literature, and it is imbued here with sensuality and violence to create an effective mirror of humanity's beastly nature. The werewolves are more basic than those found these days in fantasy fiction: there are no silver bullets, and they don't have special powers beyond the strength of the animal they become. But these werewolves are horrifying enough and drive Elena's inner conflict as she must reconcile herself to her violent nature. There is great chemistry between Clay and Elena, but also a lot of pain and betrayal, and watching them figure out if they have a way forward is great for romance fans that like a *big* conflict as well as a hero you really can't bring home to Mother.

READING PATHS

If you like the werewolves and want a romance:

Shiver by Maggie Stiefvater

If you like the werewolves and want more horror:

Frostbite by David Wellington

Warm Bodies by Isaac Marion

I have included a teen title in this category, as there is seemingly no romantic pairing too impossible for a teen romance to tackle. To prove that point, *Warm Bodies* takes a seemingly off-putting romantic premise—a zombie who falls for a human girl—and manages to tell a touching and sweet love story. At the start of this postapocalyptic story, zombie R eats the brain of a human teen and absorbs his memories, including the memories and romantic feelings the boy had for his girlfriend, Julie. R then rescues Julie from the other zombies and takes her to the airport where they hide out in an abandoned 747. R is feeling emotions he thought he never would again, and Julie is scared but curious about R once she realizes he's not going to hurt her. This romance has more obstacles than most, and even as R becomes more human, the dangers of the world they live in are still real and deadly. If ever there were a horror monster that I would have said couldn't be made romantic, it would have been a rotting zombie. But this unique horror twist on Romeo and Juliet will warm readers' hearts.

READING PATHS

If you like a story about personal transformation of the human kind and want romance:

The Accidental Bride by Jane Feather

If you like the attempt at humans and zombies living together and want horror:

Brains by Robin Becker

Blood Brothers by Nora Roberts (SIGN OF SEVEN, BOOK 1)

Cal, Fox, and Gage were best friends on a 10th-birthday sleepover trip to the woods when they swore a blood oath and unwittingly unleashed an evil force on the small town of Hawkins Hollow. Every seven years since that night, the same evil returns, wreaking havoc and causing violent outbursts among the townspeople, and the three friends seem to be the only ones who have power over the demonic force. They are coming up on the fateful anniversary, now 21 years later, and this time it looks like the evil is stronger than ever and even Cal and his friends won't be able to hold it back. Luckily they are not alone. Quinn Black has come to Hawkins Hollow to research a book on the supernatural occurrences that have plagued the town. The occult forces are coming early and stronger than ever, and somehow Quinn sees them as well. Quinn and Cal have an instant connection that soon turns romantic. They complement each other and have sparks galore, but the danger they are facing is never far from their minds. The book is part of one of Roberts's romantic trilogies, and we get hints that Fox and Gage will be getting their own love connections in the other books of the series. It also means that the final showdown with the evil force will have to wait, but for fans of Roberts, that's part of the pleasure.

READING PATHS

If you like a couple who come together to fight a curse and want romance: *The Darkest Night* by Gena Showalter

If you like the story of recurring evil in a small town and want more horror: *The Thirteen* by Susie Moloney

Romance/Mystery

One of the trickiest things in finding blends to recommend for a romance fan is finding the right balance. While blends can bring great variety to the genre and broaden its appeal beyond the core romance audience, you don't want to lose that core appeal of sparks and attraction and chemistry. With blends that involve romance and mystery you often get great sleuthing couples, but if there is not a tidy happily-ever-after ending will the romance reader be satisfied? I think the answer is that it depends. If you have readers who like series and are willing to delay their happily ever after in exchange for chemistry and the promise of an *eventual* happy ending, there are some awesome blends waiting for them. The romance plot typically revolves around throwing two people together to watch how they meet and fall for each other. The focus usually stays fairly tight on this couple, and although you can add interesting plot elements to create conflict and reasons to delay your couple's happy ending, you need to spend time with the hero and heroine. This is no less true in a satisfying romance blend. With a lot of romance/mystery blends the author starts with the mystery, and the soon-to-be-happy couple often meet over a dead body, as unromantic as that may seem. The sparks may fly right away, but there is a crime to solve and that determines a lot of how the plot is laid out. With these blends, you still need to spend time with your potential romantic couple (and spend time with them *together*), but it's the mystery plot that usually delays their happy ending and creates conflict. After they meet and the reader gets clued in that there is some sexual chemistry potential between these two, the mystery plot can unfold with its own formula pretty much intact (crime, investigation, resolution), and will often form the heart of the conflict that keeps the couple from being together. A dead body in the middle of the room will probably cool your ardor right down! If romance is a significant part of a blended book, the couple will keep being drawn together despite the obstacles that are present. The only potential issue with the mystery being blended into a romance is that there is a strong emphasis on series, which means readers will not always get a completely tidy romantic ending at the end of any one story. In this sense, they are more slavish to the mystery formula: the crime is almost always resolved in the traditional sense of the guilty party being identified and punished. But having the romance drawn out over several books, as is common in mystery/romance blends, doesn't make the relationship part of the story any less interesting—it just makes that delicious sexual tension last longer.

Silent in the Grave by Deanna Raybourn
(LADY JULIA GREY, BOOK 1)

When Lady Julia Grey's husband dies during a dinner party, she is sad but not surprised. Edward Grey had been sick for years, so when private enquiry agent Nicholas Brisbane comes to Julia and tells her that he believes her husband was murdered, she dismisses him angrily. Months later, adjusting to her new widowhood, Julia finds evidence that Nicholas may have been right and asks him to help find her husband's killer. Julia's ability to investigate is hampered by the strict rules of society in the Victorian era, especially for a young widow, but she consistently proves resourceful and determined. Nicholas is dark and brooding and slightly mysterious, so it is inevitable that an attraction blooms between the two, despite some prickly exchanges. The mystery is a good one, tight and twisty with colorful red herrings like gypsies and grave robbers. But those hoping for a sexy bed romp should not look to this series. Although there is great chemistry and Julia and Nicholas work (and fight) well together, in this first series there are too many complications and obstacles to them being together. Romance fans should not despair, as the book ends with a promise that Nicholas and Julia will meet again.

READING PATHS

If you like the couple who meet over murder and want a historical romance:

No True Gentleman by Liz Carlyle

If you like the Victorian society setting and want a mystery:

The Cater Street Hangman by Anne Perry

Welcome to Temptation by Jennifer Crusie

Sophie Dempsey is the responsible one in a family of con artists who travels to Temptation, Ohio, to help old friend Clea restart her acting career. Clea is from Temptation and wants to use the town as the setting for an audition film. Things get complicated in the small town right away when Sophie meets the mayor, sexy Phin Tucker. The two have great heat and fabulous banter, but they know Sophie will leave when the project is done. When Zane, Clea's estranged husband, follows her to Temptation, he makes a lot of threats, causes a lot of trouble, and then ends up dead. Sophie and her sister go with their Dempsey instincts and try to hide the body, but it is soon found and suspicion falls on quite a few people in town, including Sophie. Crusie is a peerless writer of romantic comedies, setting up all the playful tension and heat around her couple and waiting until halfway through the book to introduce the murder. This works on a lot of levels, most important of which is that it gives the reader a really good chance to become emotionally invested in Sophie and Phin before throwing the seemingly insurmountable obstacle of a dead body into their path to love. Lots of people had reason to want Zane dead (he was maced, drugged, shot, drowned, and then run over not once, but twice), and the mystery, despite arriving so late on the scene, is satisfying. But mostly, readers will want it cleared up so that we can get back to Phin and Sophie, who are sexy and funny and completely meant to be.

READING PATHS

If you like the strong heroine, humor, and family issues and want romance:

Natural Born Charmer by Susan Elizabeth Phillips

If you like the lighthearted tone and quirky characters and want a mystery:

Metro Girl by Janet Evanovich

Flirting with Danger by **Suzanne Enoch** (ADDISON/JELLICOE, BOOK 1)

Samantha Jellicoe and Rick Addison have a "meet cute" that is hard to beat: she breaks into his mansion to steal a rare stone tablet, gets caught by Rick, and then saves his life when a security guard hits a trip wire that sets off a bomb. Although Sam is an expert cat burglar, she didn't set the bomb that ended up killing the guard and didn't even get away with the tablet. So who did? Before she gets framed for murder, Sam asks Rick to help clear her name. He agrees not only because he owes her his life, but also because he finds her incredibly hot. Sam is suspicious and used to outwitting everyone around her. Rick has no trouble keeping up, but the man who is coolly ruthless in the boardroom has to decide how to handle the unrepentant criminal element of Sam's nature. The two grow closer as they try to find out who has it in for Rick, but things get complicated when it looks like the target might have been Sam after all. The ritzy world of Palm Beach is a fun setting for this lighter-than-air blend. The mystery is well plotted, with hints and switches and a tension-filled climax to reveal the bad guy. But what will draw readers back to the series is the winning couple who showcase opposites attracting big-time, with witty dialogue and sexual chemistry galore.

READING PATHS

If you like the female thief and opposites attracting and want a romance:

A Loving Scoundrel by Johanna Lindsey

If you like the murder plot involving a millionaire and want a mystery:

Murder Most Frothy by Cleo Coyle

Romance/Science Fiction

A great way to vary a romance is to add a new and interesting frame. Love stories are also some of our oldest stories, and it might seem sometimes like every way to explore romance has been done. But what if there were a way to explore new worlds while still telling a love story? In other words, to boldly go where no man has gone before. . . . The brawny, brainy genre of science fiction sometimes shows its feminine side. Although it started mostly as a genre written by men and read by men, that hasn't been true for a while. Now not only do we have fabulous women writing science fiction, but lots of ladies read the stuff—and not just the books written by their own gender. Although SF that appeals to women doesn't need to have a love story in it, women are like any reader—they like to see themselves in the stories they read. Finding novels from the early days of SF that deal with women's lives and emotions is not an easy task, but once these stories started appearing it was obvious that there was a market for them, and now there is a small but healthy subgenre of romantic SF. Adding a romance to science fiction doesn't have to mean that the science is less exacting or that the writer can't still explore big ideas. It simply means that the hero and heroine will have out-of-this-world conflicts.

Scout's Progress by Sharon Lee and Steve Miller
(Liaden universe, book 2)

Despite her brilliant mathematical skills, Aelliana Caylon has long been bullied and dominated by her older brother, who is heir to the head of her clan. Desperate to get out from under her family's brutal thumb, Aelliana takes a gamble—literally. She enters a card game with her meager savings and wins a starship. Meanwhile, Daav is the head of one of the most powerful clans on Liad, the Korval, but he escapes the pressures of his position by working as a mechanic at the yard where Aelliana has her ship. Although Daav has promised to wed another as part of a responsibility to shore up alliances for his clan, he finds himself spending time with Aelliana, helping her, and of course eventually loving her. Lee and Miller skillfully bring these two characters together, allow them to appreciate each other on many more levels than purely romantic, and then throw huge and terrifying obstacles in the path of their relationship. It works as a romance because you get to spend some quality time in these characters' heads and root for them completely. The SF elements of the story are also extremely well done. Not only do we get real conversations about the math and physics of space travel, it is a great work of cultural SF in which readers are introduced to a human culture very different from our own, with strict notions of loyalty and propriety.

READING PATHS

If you like the alien culture and spaceships and want romance:

The Complete Ivory by Doris Egan

If you like the struggle of a woman to find a new life and want SF:

Crystal Singer by Anne McCaffrey

Gabriel's Ghost by Linnea Sinclair (DOCK FIVE, BOOK 1)

Chasidah "Chaz" Bergren was a respected ship captain before a rigged trial put her on the prison planet of Moabar. When a monstrous genetically engineered creature called a jukor attacks her, her salvation comes from an unexpected source. She thought that her old enemy Gabriel Sullivan was dead, but suddenly Sully was right in front of her, saving her life and smuggling her off the planet. Sully wants Chaz's help to shut down the secret breeding program to create the jukors, hoping to use her knowledge of fleet operations to get them to the government labs. Chaz and Sully have sparks galore, and it's a pleasure to watch the strong-willed couple go from adversaries to lovers. But Sully has secrets and abilities that make it difficult for Chaz to trust him, and their mission is fraught with peril. The details of Sinclair's world building are interesting, with humans and other alien species interacting somewhat uneasily. Her descriptions of shipboard life and the tension of an attack at the lab will appeal to SF fans, but it is mostly the wary coming together and pulling away of the strong characters of Chaz and Sully that make this a good blend for romance fans.

READING PATHS

If you like the enemies-into-lovers trope and want a romance:

After the Night by Linda Howard

If you like the futuristic story of genetic engineering and want SF:

Falling Free by Lois McMaster Bujold

Darkship Thieves by Sarah Hoyt (DARKSHIP, BOOK 1)

Athena Sinestra is traveling with her father on their luxurious space cruiser when she is attacked and must flee for her life. Her escape pod is picked up by one of the legendary darkship raiders, but has she jumped from the frying pan into the fire? Kit and his clan live as energy-stealing pirates on the fringes of space, exiled from human society because of their genetic enhancements. There is an attraction between Kit and Athena despite their differences, and once Athena learns how many lies she has been told about the raiders and about her own people she wants to help him and his people. Athena is a tough, kick-ass heroine who doesn't make a habit of needing a rescue. She's more likely to be the one you have to be rescued *from*. And Kit is a dreamy hero: handsome, funny, and able to get into Athena's head (literally). A space opera in the grandest sense, the action of *Darkship Thieves* is nearly constant, but it also has great humor, likeable characters, and some chewy, big ideas. The romantic relationship that develops between Athena and Kit is slow burning and often hilarious but ultimately sweet and satisfying.

READING PATHS

If you like the love story between humans and aliens and want romance:

Contact by Susan Grant

If you like culture clash between human and alien and want SF:

Foreigner by C. J. Cherryh

WORKING WITH ROMANCE BLENDS

Romance, like many other genres, has a bad reputation among the literary cognoscenti as being poorly written, formulaic, escapist fare. The people that look down their noses at the genre have almost invariably never read a single romance. The truth is that *every* genre has good and bad writing, and *every* genre (even the "genre" of literary fiction) has certain elements that recur in the story lines. Sadly, it seems like the special scorn that gets heaped on romance might be at least in part because it is a genre written and read largely by women. If a reader is willing to try a romance but is put off by the covers or doesn't want to be seen browsing the romance shelves, she can get a good idea of the quality of writing in the genre by trying a romance blend. The books in this chapter all contain good examples of compelling love stories that also have interesting framing narratives. One of the big questions to ask when working with romance blends, especially if the reader doesn't normally read in the genre, is how much sex the reader is comfortable with. The romance genre (including the blends here) is mostly about getting that lead couple together. Sometimes this just means a lot of significant smoldering glances and a kiss or two, but sometimes things get a lot friskier. Readers who prefer the door to be closed on bedroom activities will want to know how graphic the love scenes are in a blend before they get a sex education class they didn't sign up for. There are some review websites that attempt to rate the explicitness of romance books (likesbooks.com is one), but it is good to keep in mind that most modern romances have a fair amount of sex.

7

SCIENCE FICTION BLENDS
Blends That Ask "What If?"

If you think science fiction is all spaceships and alien species suitable only for 14-year-old boys, you've got it wrong. Science fiction is the genre of ideas. It's full of big ideas spanning universes and smaller ones about how technology changes our lives. In a very real sense the *idea* of a science fiction novel comes first. But it is not enough to throw around "what ifs"; the important part of science fiction is to look at how ideas affect real people. High-concept stories without truthful characters give you a book that has no heart. Whether the concepts being explored affect galaxies or just one person, both have the ability to be chock-full of both wonder and humanity. The science fiction genre has been with us for a long time, and as our society became more enmeshed with emerging technology, there were writers thinking about where that technology could take us. Science fiction has its roots in the 19th-century works of Jules Verne, H. G. Wells, and a host of other writers who looked around them at the changes their society was undergoing due to scientific and technological advances and asked, "What next?" As the pace of invention and technology speeds ever faster, it is sometimes hard to know where science fiction leaves off and reality begins.

There is, of course, a reason the genre has "science" in its name. From the earliest stories, most science fiction is rooted in the questions of where science and technology are headed. This can be forecasting just a few years or many millennia into our future and imagining what might be different. The crucial thing when trying to determine whether a book is science fiction comes down to whether the world described is possible, based on what we know of the universe. Science fiction can bend the rules of science to serve the story, but if it veers too far into worlds that cannot be explained or rationalized with science, then we have left the genre and strayed into fantasy. But while that seems limiting, remembering how little we really know about our universe, one sees that the *possibilities* of science leave us with a huge palette of ideas to paint with. Do we know how life would evolve on other planets? No. But starting from principles of genetic adaptation and evolution, an author can imagine any number of alien creatures that could be out there, just waiting to be discovered.

APPEAL OF SCIENCE FICTION

The endless possibilities draw readers to science fiction. It is an imaginative genre in which authors can take a single concept and go in infinite directions. The thought that our future could include creatures and wonders and worlds nothing like our own is immensely appealing to readers of science fiction. But the fact that it is grounded in science and what is possible makes it more attractive to some than an outright fantasy story line could ever be. The science gives the story rules—malleable rules, perhaps, but rules just the same. Many science fiction fans place a high value on the technological grounding of an author. They want to know that the writer has not only put a spaceship on stage, but that she has thought about the propulsion systems, gravity, and life systems of that spaceship. The details of how the spaceship works don't all have to be there on the page, but if there is a gap, or a magical waving of hands to cover the lack of technological details, there are readers who will notice. And if the science is wrong, they will *definitely* notice! The degree to which a reader would like the technology explained to them is one of the main differences in the SF subgenres. Some hard SF requires a grounding in quantum theory. Other varieties of SF gloss over the details, and while never outright betraying the science, they might not get bogged down with how the ship flies. It just does.

All science fiction, whether hard or soft, gives the author a chance to tell stories that reflect society through the prism of the "what if?" premise. The big idea of an SF story might be the hook that grabs a reader, but if the story doesn't have humanity it will not resonate. Characters that readers can relate to are crucial to SF. The more out there the premise for a novel, the more important it seems to have a point-of-view character that a reader can bond with, empathize with, and walk in the shoes of. The protagonist's eyes are how they are going to encounter these alien worlds and futuristic technologies. Having vivid, relatable characters makes even the wildest scenarios more approachable. The core ideas that are at the heart of many science fiction stories—what it means to be human, how we relate to our environment, how we treat people who are different, how we adapt to change—could be too didactic, too heavy-handed if they were told in a present-day realistic story. It is the distance granted by the SF frame that allows these big topics to be handled lightly. Having the story filtered through an alien world, a spaceship hurtling through space, or a postapocalyptic setting gives you a new way to address those big ideas.

WHY BLEND?

The scientific underpinnings of SF mean that this can be an intimidating genre for the uninitiated. Blends with SF tend to take a slightly more laid-back approach to the science, which is helpful for those looking for a gentler entry point to the genre. Although there is a wider acceptance of SF by movie and TV audiences, written SF still can seem as if it is a genre for self-identified geeks and nerds. Science fiction, with its collectors and conventions, can seem like a club that most readers don't have a membership card for. Blending in another genre can be like a guest pass to that club. Bringing in the fan bases from other genres through a judicious blend is a great way to expose new readers to the sheer variety and wonder that can be found in science fiction. Few genres induce a more knee-jerk negative reaction than SF, and that is usually due to preconceived notions about what science fiction is and who reads it. While in other chapters we have highlighted some excellent gateway books to SF, in which the blend starts from a different genre fan base, in this chapter the books are more solidly science fiction. But the genres being added to the mix bring their own appeal to the party and can make the resulting blends an easier sell to the SF resistant. The blends can also be enjoyable for the core readers of science fiction as a new way to play with the tropes and conventions of more than one genre.

THE BLENDS

Science Fiction/Adrenaline

The science fiction genre has always had a strong tradition of publishing not only thoughtful intellectual exercises, but also rip-roaringly exciting adventure stories. Sometimes those are even found in the same book. The action-oriented SF books from authors like Robert Heinlein have crossover appeal to fans of mainstream adventure. Many of the SF books written for teens also have a high adventure quotient. There are countless books in the SF canon that are adventure stories with a space frame. A spaceship adventure can appeal to the same readers who might enjoy a nautical adventure and often even share a similar vocabulary. Whether that kind of blend appeals depends on why they read adventure stories—for the details of the frame (Old West, Navy SEALs, or futuristic starships) or for the experience of the action. But there are also blends of adrenaline and SF in which the author takes a purely science fictional premise and adds the pacing, peril, and rush of thrillers and suspense. Because the SF genre has so much variety, adrenaline blends can also vary widely. A touch of near-future tech is incredibly common in thrillers, where authors envision the next danger, the new terror. Does this make every thriller with futuristic technology science fiction? Maybe by a strict definition, but usually not by any rule book used in book publishers' marketing departments. When the technology or setting is so different that the reader will stop and think "what would that be like?" I think you have crossed into SF. Adding adrenaline genre elements to SF is a great way to get readers past any hiccups they might hit with the science bits. A brisk pace and a compelling story line will propel readers who don't care about how the tech works right into the story. The adrenaline genre can be just what it sounds like: a shot that makes your heart race, your pulse pound, and your palms sweat as you cannot *wait* to find out what happens next. Add that to a "what if?" story line, and you get stories that take you to new and exotic worlds where the stakes are high and the action is nonstop.

Neuromancer by **William Gibson** (Sprawl Trilogy, book 1)

> *Neuromancer* is the granddaddy of the cyberpunk subgenre that was big in the 1980s and 1990s. Gibson has long specialized in near-future stories, and his recent work is only barely classified as SF due to how closely his worlds resemble our own. But back when the Internet was an infant, he wrote this, his first novel. As *Neuromancer* opens, computer hacker Case has been caught stealing from his employers. They infect his brain with a toxin that prevents him from accessing cyberspace (a term Gibson coined). Case will do anything to undo the damage and get back in the game, but the price might be higher than he thinks. The shadowy conspiracies and corporations that Case struggles against for much of the book will be familiar to many thriller

fans, and the plot mirrors many dark heist thrillers. There is a noir sensibility, especially in its evocative sense of place and the banality of the violence and the dialogue. Although cyberpunk as a subgenre has faded and evolved, *Neuromancer* was highly influential for a generation of SF writers and is still a great look at a possible gritty plugged-in future.

READING PATHS

If you like the cyberpunk exploration of future tech and want something more SF:

Altered Carbon by Richard K. Morgan

If you like the antihero and heist aspects and want more of a thriller:

Nobody Runs Forever by Richard Stark

Old Man's War by John Scalzi (OLD MAN'S WAR, BOOK 1)

Of subgenres of science fiction, military space operas are often extremely action focused. One of the founding fathers of military SF is Robert Heinlein, especially when he was writing for younger audiences as with his book *Starship Troopers*. John Scalzi has admitted to playing on the pattern laid down by Heinlein, but he managed to go beyond that inspiration to develop a new space-opera universe, where he has set multiple best-selling novels. In the first, *Old Man's War*, we learn that Earth has a surplus of senior citizens and a shortage of soldiers to fight all the hostile alien races trying to chase us out of space and back to our own ball of mud. The solution that the Colonial Defense Force (CDF) has come up with is to convince aging Earthers to join the army. Their minds are transferred to new bodies pumped full of genetic enhancements and handy technology, and they are sent off to war. Scalzi takes us along with recruit John Perry as he leaves everything he knows behind to fight the CDF's wars: going through basic training, fighting his first battles, and even a little romance. It is a story that packs a lot of action and excitement but also subtly manages to explore issues of aging, loss, humanity, and the futility of war. The battle scenes will satisfy those who like thoughtful military fiction with a hefty dose of wry humor. And the examination of where technology can take us and how it will affect our humanity is pure SF.

If you like the military aspects in a space setting and want more SF:

The Forever War by Joe Haldeman

If you like the action but you're looking for more straightforward military adventure:

Semper Fi by W. E. B. Griffin

Starfish by Peter Watts (Rifter series, book 1)

When the technology is so far advanced that you don't feel you need to double-check whether it already exists, you're probably looking at science fiction. The tinkering that humans as a species tend to do with themselves, their environment, and their tech is prime territory for adrenaline books in that there are almost always unintended consequences. *Starfish* takes the idea of advances in technology that allow corporations to set up deep-sea stations, manned by specially selected and bioengineered crew members who share a certain personality type, to harness the geothermal energy at the bottom of the ocean. Unfortunately, the personality type suited for this work is highly unstable, and we follow a crew becoming more and more altered by their environment. There is a slow acceleration to the pacing in *Starfish* that shows us the tensions building as the crew changes, making this appealing to fans of psychological suspense. It also has great rewards for those SF fans who like to imagine where our technological and biological experimentation might take us and what it means to be human.

If you like the exploration of the consequences of human modification but want more SF:

Beggars in Spain by Nancy Kress

If you like the deep-sea setting and want more adrenaline suspense:

Meg by Steve Alten

Science Fiction/Fantasy

The genres of science fiction and fantasy are lumped together in many ways: by publishers, by critics, and by those who don't know much about the genres. In fact, in many libraries science fiction and fantasy are shelved together, interfiled and intermingled. Those writing about the genres often group them together under the umbrella of "speculative fiction." This is at least in part because they are seen as having a similar fan base: those looking for a reading experience that strays beyond the boundaries of the real. But there are also some real advantages in this concatenation when it comes to the many authors who have one foot in the fantasy genre and one in science fiction. The differences between SF and fantasy are numerous, but they come down to whether the world and events of a book are possible (science fiction) or impossible (fantasy). The two genres butt up against each other when the world described includes tropes popular to SF, such as technology or spaceships, but adds in elements from fantasy's impossible wheelhouse like ESP, magic, or science so advanced that it seems like magic. The advantages for writers (and readers) of SF that has fantasy blended in is that the stories are grounded in reality but still get to have some flights of fancy. Science fiction can be deadly serious at times, but the whimsy and magic of fantasy can add a hopeful lightness. Of course not all fantasy is unicorns and pixie dust, and the high-stakes struggles between good and evil can be an interesting addition to the rationality of science fiction. Knowing whether a reader is open to things that stray beyond the border of a possible future is key to whether you can suggest a science fantasy blend.

Heir to the Empire by Timothy Zahn (THRAWN, BOOK 1)

The Star Wars films and the fiction spun off from them seem on first glance to be science fiction all the way. But when you look closer, there are major parts of the Star Wars universe that look to fantasy. The most obvious of these is the magical Jedi mojo known as "The Force." Although there has been some effort to science up The Force by explaining that it is midi-chlorians in the blood that allow some to use this power, in the original movies and most of the books it is pure magic. But it is not just The Force that puts the Star Wars universe in the science fantasy arena. The stories are inherently and explicitly about good versus evil, and that is a very fantasy-like characteristic. In the first of a trilogy that many consider the best of the Star Wars tie-in novels, *Heir to the Empire* explores what happened to Han, Luke, and Leia after the defeat of the Empire in the movie *Return of the Jedi*. There is a new power trying to bring back the iron rule of the Empire, and the book explores the dark mirrors to the Jedi: the evil Sith warriors.

Although there are spaceships and planets and aliens galore, the epic nature of the struggle of light and dark will also resonate with fans of high fantasy.

READING PATHS

If you enjoy the good-versus-evil themes but want more SF:

Ender's Game by Orson Scott Card

If you like the tech underpinnings but want something that reads like fantasy:

The Gunslinger by Stephen King

The Bloody Sun by Marion Zimmer Bradley (DARKOVER, BOOK 3)

When a novel spends all its narrative time on one imaginative world and that world is filled with unusual magical abilities, it would be easy to classify that novel as fantasy. But if the author of the novel claims it instead as science fiction, what can you do? Marion Zimmer Bradley's novels set on the planet Darkover are very easy to mistake for fantasy. There is a pseudo-medieval feudal society, sword and sorcery action, and a ruling class with special magical (well, in this case telepathic) abilities. But Bradley has explained that Darkover is a lost human colony whose stranded inhabitants developed psionic abilities to adapt to their environment; hence all of Darkover is science fiction. For SF fans, some of the more appealing volumes will be those where the lost colony is rediscovered by the rest of humanity, and we have stories of recontact and culture clash. Volumes like *The Bloody Sun* concentrate on that clash and give it a personal focus, in this case in the person of a young man born on Darkover and raised on Earth. Jeff Kerwin is drawn to Darkover but soon finds he doesn't fit in there any more than he did on Earth. As he explores the secrets of the Matrix towers where Darkover adepts use psychic power, he is also searching for his own identity. The secret-heir-to-power story line is classic fantasy, but the clash of technological and more primitive societies is a great SF plot. This book (especially in its slightly rewritten later rerelease) and others of the recontact Darkover books show Bradley's skill with both genres.

READING PATHS

If you like the exploration of psychic powers but prefer SF:

The Rowan by Anne McCaffrey

If you like the clash of magic and tech but want more of a fantasy:

Tinker by Wen Spencer

Keeping It Real by **Justina Robson** (QUANTUM GRAVITY, BOOK 1)

Fairy tales are some of our oldest stories, and many of those early tales dealt with how our world and Faerie interact. That interaction is given a whole new twist by Justina Robson in this first book of her series that features an unusual combination of fairies, elves, and rock 'n' roll. After Lila Black was nearly killed while on a diplomatic mission to the Elf homelands, her injuries required extensive cybernetic replacements. These tech changes have given her an edge as she takes on a new mission in the entourage of Zal, an Elf who has taken the unheard of step of living in the human realm and performing in a rock band. Her job is to protect Zal, who has been receiving death threats, but she becomes embroiled in interdimensional politics, romance, and wild magic games. Robson manages to play extensively with the canon of fairy in a completely original yet respectful way, and her addition of cyborgs and SF trappings adds an original edge to her fast-paced adventure.

READING PATHS

If you like the multiple-dimension travel with more of an SF feel:

Time's Eye by Arthur C. Clarke and Stephen Baxter

If you like the interplay of humans and Fey but are looking for a fantasy:

Little, Big by John Crowley

Science Fiction/Historical Fiction

It would seem a completely oxymoronic endeavor to write a book that mixed the forward-looking, futurist genre of science fiction with a genre that wallows in the details and landscapes of the past. How would that even work? It turns out it can work really well in the hands of an author with an appreciation for both genres. Sometimes this might involve a historical setting and imagining how the people in that setting would adapt to a science fictional encounter. It could involve the science fiction trope of time travel so you could perhaps start in the future and use technology to travel to the past. But there is also a whole subgenre of science fiction that deals with reimaginings of historical time periods. This subgenre of alternative history gets classed (and rightly so) with science fiction because at the core it is a "what if?" story. Yes, history is heavily referenced but usually through a slightly different prism. When successfully blended, an SF/historical pairing can look at the possibilities of the future through the lens of the past. Both genres have a strong tradition of writing about how individuals can change the future. They are both interested in building a world for the reader, although one is based on the actual facts of the past and the other is inked with the possibilities of the future. In a great blend, the landscape and setting details that so appeal to historical fiction fans can be yoked to a nifty piece of speculation for an even stronger story.

Eifelheim by Michael Flynn

There are many stories in science fiction of what first contact with an alien culture would be like, but most are told in the present day of the author and deal with the reactions of modern people. In *Eifelheim*, we learn about life in a small village in 14th-century Germany and imagine how its residents might deal with an alien encounter. One day an extraterrestrial ship crashes in the nearby forest, and villagers including local priest Father Dietrich go to the aid of the shipwrecked aliens. Described as looking like giant grasshoppers, the aliens and their advanced technology should have caused absolute panic. But they are lucky in their first contact, as Dietrich is a remarkably open-minded man, highly educated and interested in natural philosophy and science. The struggles of the villagers to understand and accept the aliens open up the story to great themes like the fear of the *other*, what charity means, and what it would be like for a technologically primitive society to encounter science so advanced as to appear to be magic. The historical setting is fleshed out with details of daily life and local politics, making it a great backdrop for this unique tale of culture clash. The struggles of the villagers to accept the aliens and the efforts of Father Dietrich to both understand them and yet still impose his own ideas of religion and morality on them are fascinating, as is the way that we get to see these aliens only from the viewpoint of people who may be enlightened for their time but are still limited by their experiences.

READING PATHS

If you like the culture clash of first contact and want more SF:

Triptych by J. M. Frey

If you like the setting of medieval Europe and want more historical fiction:

The Sunne in Splendour by Sharon Kay Penman

Blackout/All Clear by Connie Willis (OXFORD SERIES, BOOKS 3 AND 4)

This pair of books set in Willis's universe of time-traveling Oxford scholars has a group of historians jumping back to various pivotal moments during WWII to observe the behavior of the English in wartime. Dangerous assignments are made even more so by strange slippages in their jumps. Are the rules of time travel being broken by repeat visits? The amazing ability that Willis has to create believable breathing characters is made more incredible by her willingness to pitch them into terrible situations. The scholars are warned not to interact with the historical events that they are observing, but events tend to overtake them and make them realize that history is made up of moments of people making choices. The first volume, *Blackout*, establishes our characters in their historical assignments, and the sequel, *All Clear*, increasingly deals with the consequences of time travel and the efforts of the historians to return home. The details of wartime England are as lovingly drawn as in any historical novel, with special attention paid to the everyday heroics of those dealing with the dangers and privations of the Blitz. The point-of-view characters are inserted into a time but not *of* that time, so they have a modern view on the history they experience.

READING PATHS

If you like the time travelers and want something more SF:

In the Garden of Iden by Kage Baker

If you like the Blitz setting and want more historical fiction:

Night Watch by Sarah Waters

Galileo's Dream by Kim Stanley Robinson

Examinations of how the past shapes the future can be found throughout SF, but rarely are they treated as literally as in this work that imagines a far-future emissary from Jupiter who travels to 17th-century Italy to consult Galileo. It seems that residents of Jupiter are having a crisis of faith, and as their society hinges on the teachings of Galileo, they send someone back to try to influence his work and ensure their own future. Although we spend time experiencing both the political debates on Jupiter and the scientific circles of Venice, it is the sections with Galileo in his own time that truly sing. Watching the scientist struggle to make sense of the future he has glimpsed while in the grip of his own discoveries is fascinating, as is his frustration to see how much of one's destiny is fixed and cannot be changed. Although Robinson does a phenomenal job drawing the character of Galileo and his time, the Jovian future frame will probably limit the appeal of this to science fiction aficionados, which seems a bit of a shame as this is obviously a meticulously researched book.

READING PATHS

If you like the use of real historical characters but want something more SF:

> *To Your Scattered Bodies Go* by Philip Jose Farmer

If you like the new view of the history of science but want something that is historical fiction:

> *Quicksilver* by Neal Stephenson

Science Fiction/Horror

Although science fiction and horror share space under the umbrella of "speculative fiction," they don't often play together. The essence of the appeal of horror is the thing in the dark, the unknown terror lurking around the corner, and the unexplainable. But science fiction likes to look in all the dark corners and explain or at least explore all the mysteries of the universe. The movie *Alien* is a classic example of how to use the creature lurking in the dark trope of horror to excellent effect in science fiction. It is a classic alien story, but the alien is so *other*, so terrifying, that the horror label fits just as easily. The emotional manipulation that horror does so well—making a reader dread and fear what is coming next—can be a nice change of pace for an intellectual genre like science fiction. Thoroughly modern stories can be given a shot of hair-raising tension by juxtaposing all the things we think we know against the things we don't. Poking our noses into things we don't understand is the way humans evolve, but there has probably been quite a lot of Darwinian selection when we poked into the wrong places. That makes for a good story. The hubris of science facing off against the unknowable horror works as a structure because we as readers like to see the downfall of the self-righteous know-it-all. And if his downfall is at the hands of a horrifying monster that he unwittingly created or spent a chunk of time saying could never exist, all the better.

The Games by **Ted Kosmatka**

Exploring the perils of embracing technology without a balancing grounding in humanity is a great SF/horror blend idea. In author Kosmatka's future, we are shown a morally bankrupt society in which there are almost no ethical checks on genetic tinkering, and engineered monstrosities fight to the death in televised gladiatorial games. Silas Williams is a geneticist usually in charge of preparing the entry for the United States in a gladiatorial Olympics in which the only rule is the contestants cannot have any human DNA. In the race to develop a better killing machine, Silas discovers that the government has turned the genetic design over to a supercomputer, but the resulting creature is soon uncontrollable. The action-packed plot has plenty of horrific gore and a very scary monster but is also deeply interested in the SF question of where technology can take us and whether we truly wish to go there.

READING PATHS

If you like the risky genetic tinkering and want SF:

Trikon Deception by Ben Bova

If you like a scary look at genetic modification and want horror:

Parasite by Mira Grant

The Stand by **Stephen King**

Postapocalyptic stories are by their speculative nature science fiction, but they get told in such a vast array of narrative styles that they can end up in fantasy, horror, science fiction, or even increasingly in literary

fiction. Where they fall can be determined by what caused the apocalypse (disease, zombies, alien invasion), but it is usually the style of
storytelling that determines whether a post-apocalypse book falls in
or out of genre. *The Stand* is one of the classic stories of the end of the
world, combining an SF premise of a runaway virus with a supernatural evil force from horror. A super flu is developed in a government lab
but escapes to ravage the globe, eventually being known as "Captain
Trips." When the disease burns itself out, the world's population is
a tiny fraction of what it was and the remnants of humanity end up
gravitating into two camps: the Free Zone led by Mother Abigail and
the group led by Randall Flagg, a man with supernatural evil powers.
Of course the setup is for a final epic battle of good and evil, but we
have lots of great SF musing on what would happen to society in the
face of catastrophe and how we might try to rebuild. Hugely important to the canon of postapocalyptic fiction, not to mention just plain
huge, *The Stand* is nevertheless a page-turner whose horror comes not
only from the supernatural evil of Flagg's Walkin' Dude, but also the
horror of regular people swayed to evil acts.

READING PATHS

If you like the superbug and want more apocalyptic SF:

The Earth Abides by George R. Stewart

If you like the postapocalyptic setting that spawns evil and want more
horror:

Bird Box by Josh Malerman

The Dry Salvages by Caitlin R. Kiernan (NOVELLA)

The idea of travel to the deep unknown regions of space is an inherently scary premise. A paleontologist with expertise on the fossils of
other planets, Audrey Cather traveled 15 light years to the moon Piros
when she was a young woman. Fifty years later she is writing down
her story because everyone else who knows what happened is dead
and the government wants her silent. Using an effective technique
of the halting narrative of a woman who wants to tell but fears to
remember, we learn Audrey's story. She and three colleagues were to
join up with the members of an earlier mission exploring the surface

of a moon, which appeared to have been abandoned by its inhabitants many ages ago. They wake from cryogenic sleep to find that everyone down on the moon is missing, and those left on the ship in orbit have succumbed to some kind of madness. Kiernan packs an amazingly intense story into this novella, with fascinating speculative elements like genetic tinkering, synthetic humanoid robots, and of course what might be out there among the stars. The tension is built skillfully with the two time periods, and as we slowly get more of a picture of what Audrey and her colleagues encounter, the level of dread escalates sharply. Sometimes there is nothing scarier than a menace that you are told about but never shown, and Kiernan's background as a horror writer shows a mastery of this technique. Your imagination and anticipation will fill in the blanks in a way that a fully fleshed-out monster described in Technicolor detail could never rival.

READING PATHS

If you like the story from the last survivor of a doomed mission and want SF:

The Sparrow by Mary Doria Russell

If you like the menace in space and want horror:

Season of Passage by Christopher Pike

Science Fiction/Mystery

Science fiction and mystery share a sense of intellectual curiosity. In mystery the focus is on the puzzle of a crime, while in science fiction the writer is delving into questions of human and technological advancement. But they both prompt readers to think about the logical consequences of a train of events. The formula of a mystery follows clues dropped by the author to help lead the reader to discover who committed the crime. The heart of a science fiction reading experience requires the reader to take the premise of a futuristic world and think about how we would get there, as well as how getting there would change us. The two genres are different but can often combine to the great enjoyment of both fan bases. The plotting of mysteries can be a great tool for other genre authors to use when they need to have the story move along with purpose. The danger of even the best science fiction is that it can drift into too much idea and not enough story. Yes, it's fascinating that an author has thought about the linguistic basis of alien languages and how their anatomy shapes the vowel formations, and, and, and . . . . But really, all the details in the world cannot substitute for a plot. In the mystery chapter I focused on blended titles that start firmly from the mystery camp. But here, I opted for titles that have a strong SF appeal plus some engaging plotting provided by the mystery genre. When a book stands more squarely in the mystery camp, that part of the story propels everything, and the SF setting, while interesting and definitely value added, is not paramount. For the blends here, you could not strip away the setting and get a plain mystery. The ideas at the heart of the stories—the big "what ifs"—are integral to the story. By mixing in a mystery to a science fiction story, you not only get to explore the science fictional world created by the author, but you also get to imagine how crime fits into that world.

Great North Road by Peter F. Hamilton

In Hamilton's remarkably built future world, humanity has been colonizing other worlds, not through space travel, but through teleportation portals. The first of these portals was opened to the planet of St. Libra and is controlled by the fabulously wealthy North family of clones. This sprawling epic actually ranges across many genres; it is a thoroughly SF setting but begins and ends with cops investigating a mystery: who killed a wealthy and important member of the North family and dumped his body in Newcastle? The action alternates away from Earth when the investigation points to an alien monster who may have committed a similar crime 20 years before on St. Libra. That is, if the monster ever existed. The story of the fast-paced hunt for the alien is balanced by the methodical police work still going on in Newcastle, although both plots are tangled with politics—both governmental and corporate. It is a complicated, long book but one with great rewards. The descriptions of how crime investigations would happen in a fully wired future give a great sense of the powerful toys cops might use, but the fact that human beings are still criminal, fallible, and corruptible grounds the future detectives and present-day readers.

READING PATHS

If you like a touch of mystery but want more of an SF alien contact story:

Leviathan Wakes by James S. A. Corey

If you like the investigatory challenges of crimes involving the rich and powerful and want a mystery:

Night Watcher by John Lutz

Caves of Steel by Isaac Asimov (ROBOT SERIES, BOOK 1)

One of the earliest SF/mystery blends still entertains both fan bases. Lije Baley is a cop in a future Earth society where we all live in hyperdense cities. He is assigned a case involving a murder in Spacetown, the port area where those who immigrated generations ago to Outer World colonies have a small Earthside presence. The murder is politically charged, due to the uneasy relationship between the colonies and Earth, and Lije is forced to take on a Spacetown partner who just happens to be a robot. Robots have been introduced on Earth, but they are crude machines compared to his new humanoid partner R. Daneel Olivaw. They are also highly resented by the Earth population who fear the loss of jobs widespread robot use might cause. As Asimov explores all of these and other great SF problems, he also portrays Lije as a very convincing cop trying to solve a nearly impossible case. The imagined future society is a typical 1950s mix of awkward wrong guesses and prescience that is as interesting for what it gets wrong as for what could still seem possible. Likewise the mystery takes several wrong turns and blind alleys but delivers a very satisfying ending, while being most interesting for the way Asimov imagines that human criminal behavior has remained with us. There is a long history of a cop hero having an "odd couple" partner to play off of, and it is especially effective here in the interplay between Lije and Daneel.

READING PATHS

If you like the interplay of human and robot and want more SF:

Software by Rudy Rucker

If you like the idea of partners from different worlds (less literally) and want a mystery:

A Great Deliverance by Elizabeth George

The Disappeared by Kristine Kathryn Rusch (RETRIEVAL ARTIST, BOOK 1)

Detectives Flint and DeRicci work in Armstrong Dome, the oldest and biggest human settlement on the moon in a future in which humanity has had centuries to develop delicate interspecies treaties with the various alien species with whom we trade. While working the port zone, they catch three cases in a row that all seem to involve humans on the run from alien justice rulings. To maintain the trade between cultures, Earth has agreed to turn over any human found guilty in an alien court, no matter how minor the infraction or unjust the ruling may be in human terms. Some of those found guilty turn to firms that specialize in making them "disappear" by giving them new identities. But some of the Disappeared are being found again on Flint and DeRicci's turf. The police work of the future seems to share a lot in common with our time: lots of coffee is consumed, a lot of paperwork is required, and while the questions of justice might be over a cop's pay grade, that doesn't mean they can be ignored. In *The Disappeared* Flint and DeRicci are new partners, and although they have a rocky start they complement each other well. The two main cases involve different alien species, and Rusch has thought about the way they might think and behave and especially about the difficulties humans might have dealing with cultures so different from our own.

READING PATHS

If you like the intercultural explorations and want something more SF:

A Fire Upon the Deep by Vernor Vinge

If you like investigators trying to balance the letter of the law against what they believe is right and want a mystery:

Gone, Baby, Gone by Dennis Lehane

Science Fiction/Romance

Science fiction started out as a boys' club. From its early beginnings most of its writers and readers were male and any female writers often hid behind pseudonyms or initials to avoid alienating the core fan base. But there was a boom in women writing in the genre that picked up speed in the 1970s and 1980s and continues to this day. A side effect of the gender balancing in SF is that portrayals of women have grown more nuanced and appealing to female readers and issues of gender relations have been addressed more readily in the genre. This does not mean that women were absent from the stories of early SF or even that women didn't read those early stories. But with more women reading and writing SF, some themes and stories that traditionally appeal to women found their way into the literature. These include romantic story lines being more prominent in the plots, more examination of gender relations, and more complex female characterization. For a book that successfully blends science fiction and romance, you need to think about what each genre brings to the party and how they can be balanced without undermining each other. Science fiction is often very plot based as the authors play with their "what if?" ideas. But the characters who populate and drive the plot need to be real to readers. A romantic story line can be the touch point for readers who aren't usually engaged by science fiction plots. The romance chapter has some great examples of romances that sprinkle in some science fiction scenery, and here I looked for stories where the love story was present and satisfying but not to the exclusion of the science.

Grimspace by Ann Aguirre (SIRANTHA JAX, BOOK 1)

It takes a very special type of person to navigate the beacons between stars; carriers of the J-gene are the only humans who can safely jump through grimspace. Sirantha Jax was a valued and respected navigator for the Farwan Corporation before she found herself locked in a holding cell, interrogated and abused by psychiatrists who wanted her to admit she caused a crash that killed a delegation of important diplomats as well as everyone else on board, even her pilot and lover, Kai. When she is unexpectedly rescued by the enigmatic March, she is given no choice but to aid them in their mission to revolt against the Corp and start an independent school for Jumpers. Things get complicated quickly, and the one complication she does not know how to handle is a growing attraction to March, a pilot who also has psi abilities. Jax is used to looking out for herself, and the push-pull between her and March has a delicious tension, especially when she realizes he is also broken and vulnerable. The politics and SF details are just being sketched in by this first volume of an ongoing series featuring Jax, but they manage to keep the reader as engaged as the romance. Far from a simple boy-meets-girl story, *Grimspace* is about the growth of Jax from a spoiled, selfish corporate tool into an independent woman with a purpose. The science here is soft, with a well-built world of space travel that nevertheless spends little time on *how* space travel works.

READING PATHS

If you like the theme of strong women bucking expectations and want more SF:

> *Song of Scarabeus* by Sara Creasy

If you like the prickly, independent heroine and emphasis on personal growth but want more romance:

> *Lead Me On* by Victoria Dahl

Shards of Honor by Lois McMaster Bujold (VORKOSIGAN SAGA, BOOK 1)

The Miles Vorkosigan books by Bujold are a wide-ranging series: always science fiction but with plotlines that encompass other genres and influences including adventure, mystery, and romance. This is one reason the series stays fresh and is eminently rereadable. The first book in the series chronologically (although not the first published) actually focuses not on height-challenged, hyperactive, scion of his house Miles Vorkosigan, but on how his parents meet. Cordelia Naismith is introduced as a young captain of a ship in the Beta Colony exploratory fleet who encounters a hostile force from the planet Barrayar when checking out a supposedly uninhabited planet. The leader of the Barrayaran force is Aral Vorkosigan, an older warrior with a fierce reputation, and there is an immediate and strong attraction between the two despite their situation. As we follow Cordelia and Aral through their adventures, we get not only an exciting space-opera plot, but also a nuanced romance between two strong-willed individuals. The Romeo/Juliet setup of enemies becoming lovers is given a galactic twist, and Bujold sets up a world that she will successfully explore in future volumes. Never treacly or sentimental, the romance here is a large element, yet not off-putting to those who do not read in the romance genre but who will want to find out how one of the great characters in SF came into the world.

READING PATHS

If you like the culture clash and want more SF:

> *Primary Inversion* by Catherine Asaro

If you like opposites attracting and want more romance:

> *Amaryllis* by Jayne Castle

The Host by Stephenie Meyer

Alien invasion and human subjugation would not seem like a great background for romance, but in Meyer's hands, we get a tender love story that still engages SF readers. Wanderer is a member of the parasitical invading alien species that have descended on Earth and taken up residence in the bodies of their human hosts. Usually the aliens take over all consciousness from their humans, but the person that Wanderer has picked puts up a fight. She is in the body of Melanie Stryder, whose will is so strong that she convinces Wanderer to seek out a pocket of human survivors that include her remaining family and her lover. The choice to have the story told from conquering invader Wanderer's point of view is a bold one that gives this alien contact story a fresh perspective. The group, who call her Wanda, eventually accepts her. Wanderer finds herself drawn to these people that her human host loved deeply, and so she experiences new emotions. Ruminating on the nature of love and what it means to be human, this unique take on alien conquest has a great soapy romantic triangle at its heart.

READING PATHS

If you like the alien/human gender relations and want more SF:

The Left Hand of Darkness by Ursula LeGuin

If you like stories of forbidden love between conqueror and conquered and want romance:

The Prize by Julie Garwood

WORKING WITH SCIENCE FICTION BLENDS

Science fiction has an immense amount of variety to it, as evidenced by the very different kinds of stories in the blended books above. If readers don't think they like SF, or if they are burned out on a particular kind of SF book, the good news is that there is something for just about everyone. By adding those other genre elements to SF, an author can open up whole new audiences. Many fear the aisles with all the spaceships on the covers, but as this chapter illustrates, those books (fun as they are) are not the only tales being told in the genre. Sometimes the publishers of books that blend in other genres still market their books squarely at the SF fan base through their choice of cover art and advertising, but you can find books that play with the big ideas of the genre hidden all around the library. Sometimes that sneak attack is a way to introduce readers to a genre they find intimidating. Books that have science fiction as part of a blend can work for reluctant readers when you can hook them on a cool idea, without selling them on the whole canon of SF. The key appeal of the genre carries through no matter what other genre is added to the mix: wonder and possibility.

8

WHOLE COLLECTION BLENDS
Looking beyond the Fiction Stacks for Blends

The idea of whole collection readers' advisory has been gaining steam in recent years. In her book *The Readers' Advisory Guide to Nonfiction*, Neal Wyatt talks about the value of thinking about readers' advisory more holistically (Wyatt 2007). The purpose of whole collection readers' advisory is to draw the connections between materials from all over our libraries for patrons. Most library users are not exclusive consumers of any one medium. They might come in for a book and leave with a film on DVD or be flipping through a graphic novel when they see a TV series they've always meant to watch. And this whole-collection consumption can happen even more easily as we build better online catalogs that serve as discovery tools. Looking up "Star Wars" in an average library's online catalog shows that patrons could check out not only the movies, but also dozens of novels (for all ages) and graphic novels set in the Star Wars universe, DVDs of the animated Clone Wars TV series, nonfiction works about the creation of the movies, and even tie-in video games. Although this is an extreme example of a media empire telling countless stories that share a fictional universe, reminding patrons that the stories they love can be told other ways is the useful thing to remember. This kind of whole-collection RA can also happen with the blends that are found throughout our libraries, not just on the fiction shelves.

In this chapter, I focus on the visual media of TV, film, and graphic novels to explore whole-collection RA with blends, but there are other parts of the collection where delightful mixing occurs. Audiobooks, like their printed parents, are a good option for those drawn to genre blends. Just like the books they are based on, they can cross any genre but with the added alchemy that a listening experience can bring. There is something about hearing a story read that can transport the listener even deeper into the book, where nuances of mood and tension can be conveyed by a good narrator. Nonfiction is usually a big part of whole-collection RA, as we try to remember to make the connections between stories that strike the same chords, whether they are fictional or not. But nonfiction has genres of its own, sometimes similar to those used in fiction, sometimes radically different. Any time you try to put things safely into categories, there will be works that straddle and bridge those categories. Even a traditionally less-narrative format like video games can get in on the blending act. Recognizable genre elements can be seen in many of the modern video games that are increasingly interested in telling a story in their interactive play. Science fiction, fantasy, horror, mystery, adventure, romance, and historical fiction are all genres that can be incorporated into games, and creators often borrow from several. Finally, it's a good idea to remember that fans of genre fiction often read above and below their "appropriate" age level in search of a good story. Teen fiction in particular has always embraced genre blending. There are almost no better examples of improbable genre blends of romance and horror than those written for teens, who seem to delight in impossible love stories.

Once readers start to look for ways to make these connections between collections, they can be found everywhere. But because our collections are usually corralled off—fiction with other fiction, the nonfiction on the other side of the building, movies on shelves far away from the books, and so on—sometimes patrons need help making those connections. Just as I discussed the challenges of getting readers to look beyond the way a book is marketed or where it is shelved when it comes to blends, the same challenges occur when making connections to other media. The biggest challenge is simply to remember to suggest a similar story that happens to come in a different kind of container. When we're talking with patrons about books, it is easy to forget that we might have other media that would also work for that patron.

WHY BLEND?

Novelists aren't the only ones who like to blend genres. In every medium that has recognizable genre elements, there are creators who enjoy mixing them up. This mixing can even be very effective in the visual media, as creators can tip their hats to an entire genre simply by lighting a scene a certain way or changing the backing score. The genres that I have highlighted in the previous chapters all also occur in other media, sometimes with their own special subgenres and variations that only appear in that medium. Just like in literature, the labels that get put on movies, TV, and graphic novels are usually mostly of interest to marketing people. Although there are times when patrons might come to the library saying they want a particular genre or category of a movie, for example, most browsers don't initially preselect like that. It also seems, as with film for example, that users are already used to talking about movies in terms of their appeal: something scary, something action-packed, something funny, and so on. Because libraries do not usually separate their DVDs or graphic novels by genre, it is likely that patrons will stumble upon a blended story in the nonbook parts of our libraries. Creators of visual media blend genres to bring together disparate audiences, broaden appeal, and take creative chances.

WORKING WITH BLENDS IN WHOLE COLLECTION RA

When working with patrons, one of the most useful ways to talk to people who are not big readers (or who are simply not used to talking about books) is to try to draw out their reading preferences by talking about the TV and films they enjoy. This works because it can get people thinking about what kinds of stories they respond to and look for again and again. Sometimes these break down along genre lines, and we can use that information as a starting place to talk about what kinds of books they might also enjoy. For example, a fan of a show like *Law & Order* might enjoy police procedurals or legal thrillers. Someone who queues up for every romantic comedy that hits theaters might also enjoy romance in their books. Just as with the blended books discussed earlier, there are many works in the visual media that borrow and blend and mix genre elements. This is where you can make some really useful cross-medium suggestions for patrons. Because these other media can seem like a small investment of time in comparison to reading an entire novel, it can be an easy way to convince a browser to try a blend that includes genres outside their normal patterns of consumption. Even those opposed to a whole genre like science fiction in books might be open to spending two hours in a visual science fiction world on film. Whether or not that will ever translate into a different opinion about the genre as a whole is unknown, but the barriers seem lower in TV and film.

TV

Episodic television has a unique ability to tell lots of different kinds of stories within the same series. While most series fall firmly into one category or genre, any series can take a small excursion to a new genre for one episode without actually changing its core audience. Part of the freedom of having a dozen or more storytelling slots each season is that creators can indulge in a little cross-genre pollination. But some TV series regularly and deliberately play in more than one genre. Which genres they choose to mix in can vary, but there are some that are used often. The continuing popularity of the police procedural TV show means that TV series continue to try to find ways to pull in fans of cop shows while pushing into other genres. Romance is another genre that gets mixed in with great frequency. Sometimes a TV series is set up with a romance dynamic built in, but in others the romance might grow over time. There is even a word for those who root for romance plots: *'shippers* (for relationshippers). The speculative genres like science fiction and fantasy get mixed into TV series for the sheer visual appeal of their imaginative worlds. But any genre can cross-pollinate on TV, gathering disparate genre fandoms together in often cult-like new fan bases.

The X-Files (1993–2002)

One of the shows that consistently pushed genre boundaries and liked to mix things up was *The X-Files*. The series starred David Duchovny as Fox Mulder, an FBI agent tasked with investigating the cases that the FBI deems too weird for other departments, and costarred Gillian Anderson as Dana Scully, his more level-headed, science-minded partner. The series showcased the special ability of episodic TV to be able to tackle radically different stories from week to week. And on *The X-Files* those stories could cover almost every genre, with horror making a frequent appearance. But two genres shared the main narrative focus on this series. Each episode often contained a mystery arc, with Mulder and Scully tackling a new case involving some sort of unexplained phenomenon or strange creature. These two are both (in their own ways) trained investigators, and the cases they tackled often included dead bodies and ended up with someone in custody, just like a mystery. But the other genre that formed the backbone of some of the longer running story lines is science fiction. Mulder believes in the existence of extraterrestrial aliens, and his search for the truth of the aliens and a possible government conspiracy to cover up their existence runs throughout the show. The genres all work together, sometimes mixing in a single episode and sometimes taking turns as the focus of a story line.

MORE MEDIA MIXES

Film with aliens and investigators: *Men in Black*

Book that mixes horror with shadowy conspiracies: *Straw Men* by Michael Marshall

Graphic novel that mixes horror and the occult: *The Chill* by Jason Starr

---

Pushing Daisies (2007–2009)

Bryan Fuller's series about a pie maker (Lee Pace) who can bring people back from the dead is a surprisingly whimsical and Technicolor mix of fantasy, mystery, and romance. Ned (when he isn't making pies) works with private investigator Emerson Cod (Chi McBride) to leverage his supernatural talent to solve mysteries. He can touch a dead person to bring him back to life, but he must touch him again before 60 seconds has elapsed or someone else will die. Once he touches the revived person a second time, the person is dead forever. Ned and Emerson have been reviving murder victims, asking them who killed them, solving the case, and splitting the reward. The rules of Ned's powers are easy to follow until he brings his childhood sweetheart, Chuck (Anna Friel), back to life and decides he wants to keep her around. The romance of the series is sweet and complicated by the fact that Ned and Chuck can never touch or she will die again permanently. The cases that Emerson and Ned (now helped by Chuck) tackle in each episode are the kind found in cozy mysteries—nothing too serious, nothing too violent. There is a great cast of eccentric characters supporting the leads and lots of witty banter and wordplay reminiscent of old screwball comedies of the 1940s. The show was canceled far too soon.

MORE MEDIA MIXES

Film that is both whimsically fantastic and romantic: *Amelie*

Book that mixes mystery, romance, and fantasy: *Truly, Madly* by Heather Webb

Graphic novel that features romantic story lines and fantasy worlds: *Fruits Basket* by Natsuki Takaya

---

Firefly (2002–2003)

Joss Whedon is the king of blending and bending genres to new and unusual purposes, most famously with *Buffy the Vampire Slayer* but also with the cult favorite SF/western/adventure series *Firefly*. In the universe of *Firefly*, there are core planets of the Alliance that have all the money, technology, and shiny toys, and then there are the outer planets where life is more primitive, low tech, and violent. Malcolm Reynolds (Nathan Fillion) was a sergeant in the rebel forces that tried to split off from the Alliance during a civil war and lost. He now captains a freighter that operates on the fringes of the galaxy, trying to stay out of Alliance attention and making a living taking on jobs of dubious legality. At the launch of the series, Mal picks up two troublesome crew members on the run from the law, an Alliance-trained doctor and the sister he rescues from a government lab. Much of the series revolves around the legal and illegal jobs that Mal and the crew take on, all usually involving a lot of action and danger, which gives the series its adventure feel. But the jobs tend to be on frontier planets that feel like they have been pulled straight out of an American western, complete with costumes and sets that evoke the Old West. And of course, the science fiction elements of a great space opera are here too. It's a combination that shouldn't work but does, mainly due to the talented ensemble cast and stellar writing. This was another show canceled after one season but hugely popular on DVD. A movie was made, *Serenity*, to capitalize on the show's post-demise popularity.

MORE MEDIA MIXES

Film that mixes westerns with SF: *Cowboy Bebop* (anime)

Book that is speculative fiction with a western vibe: *Gunslinger* by Stephen King

Graphic novel with aliens in the Old West: *Cowboys & Aliens* by Scott Mitchell Rosenberg

MORE TV GENRE BLENDS

Grimm (horror/fantasy/mystery)

True Blood (romance/horror/fantasy)

The Prisoner (SF/adventure/thriller)

Lost (SF/fantasy/adventure/romance)

Doctor Who (SF/fantasy/adventure/historical)

Quantum Leap (SF/historical)

Beauty and the Beast (romance/fantasy/mystery)

Life on Mars (SF/mystery)

Film

Compared to many other narrative forms, movies have a relatively short amount of time to pack in a story. Two hours, three tops, and the creators have to get everything they want to say onto the screen. The fact that it is even possible is part of the magic of movies. Script and acting, lighting and sound, sets and costumes, they all combine to paint a picture that would take many times as long to tell in words. Genres are as much a part of filmmaking as they are of written books, with the same kinds of dependable elements and built-in expectations. And filmmakers, just like authors, sometimes like to mix and borrow and blend genre elements together for new and different results. Some genres get used and borrowed more than others. The adrenaline genres in film could be translated to action, adventure, thriller, and suspense and are all perennially popular, reliably packing in audiences looking for fast-paced popcorn movies. Adrenaline could be said to be the element you add to a movie to bring in the guys. Romance also appears both alone and as a reliable blending element and is often how you try to get more women to see a movie. The mystery genre was so popular and stylized in the noir films of the 1940s that blends that use mystery to this day often borrow noir elements. Science fiction tends to automatically get blended with action/adrenaline in Hollywood movies (rare low-key exceptions exist like Duncan Jones's *Moon*) and could be stretched to include the very popular comic book adaptations that come out with great regularity. Of course, depending on how you look at those, they could be classed as fantasy as well. Historical usually gets an opulent epic treatment on film, and horror gets teens into theater seats. The blending can be done in film for the same reasons authors blend in books: to have fun, dabble in a genre the creator loves, and add an interesting frame.

Blade Runner (DIRECTED BY RIDLEY SCOTT)

Not particularly successful when it was released in 1982, this science fiction/noir mystery blend gained a cult following that remains strong to this day. Set in a dystopian futuristic Los Angeles that includes flying cars, omnipresent advertising, and lifelike androids called replicants, the story revolves around a hunt for four rogue replicants who are on Earth looking for their creator. Former cop Rick Deckard (Harrison Ford) was the best blade runner the LAPD ever had, hunting down the replicants who are used as labor in the off-planet colonies but are forbidden on Earth. He gets tagged to retire the four fugitives, a hunt that includes plenty of action, and even some romance when Deckard meets the experimental replicant Rachael (Sean Young), an android who thinks she's human. The burnt-out cop convinced to take one final case is a classic mystery premise, but *Blade Runner*'s explicitly noir elements include the lighting (and shadows), costumes, and retro/futuristic score. In addition to the gorgeous future-noir look of the film's LA, there are intriguing SF ideas at play here, including what it means to be human. This was *very* loosely based on Philip K. Dick's book *Do Androids Dream of Electric Sheep?*

MORE SF/NOIR MEDIA MIXES

TV: *Dark Angel*

Book: *VN* by Madeline Ashby

Graphic novel: *Akira* by Katsuhiro Otomo

Raiders of the Lost Ark (DIRECTED BY STEVEN SPIELBERG)

Although it was made in the 1980s, this first of the Indiana Jones movies is a conscious throwback to adventure movies of an earlier age. Set in the 1930s, *Raiders of the Lost Ark* stars Harrison Ford as archaeologist Indiana Jones, lecturer and treasure hunter. The movie opens with a hugely entertaining nonstop action sequence in which Jones is attempting to retrieve a golden idol from a cave in the Salvadoran jungle. He gets the idol, only to have it taken from him by archnemesis and Nazi treasure hunter Belloq and ends up being chased by native tribesman, escaping by the skin of his teeth. Action then shifts to the Middle East and the search for the legendary Ark of the Covenant. The Nazis want the Ark too, but Jones knows where to find a medallion that seems to be the key to the Ark's location. It's a little awkward that the medallion's current owner is old flame Marion Ravenwood (Karen Allen), but the two team up on the hunt for the Ark. The biggest draw of *Raiders* is undoubtedly the thrill ride of constant danger and near escapes, but the historical setting, excellent bad guys in the rival Nazi treasure hunters, and the rekindling of romance between Marion and Indy also have great appeal. Three other films have been made in the franchise, but none can match the charm and originality of the first, which combines historical action, humor, and romance into one irresistible package.

MORE MEDIA MIXES

TV that has the adventure and exotic locales of Indiana Jones movies: *Alias*

Book with *Raiders*-like action: *Sahara* by Clive Cussler

Graphic novel with a resourceful hero like Indiana Jones: *The Rocketeer* by Dave Stevens

---

The Princess Bride (DIRECTED BY ROB REINER)

A hilarious twist on a classic fairy tale, *The Princess Bride* has something for everyone. Set in a traditional medieval fantasy world, the central story is of princess bride Buttercup (Robin Wright) and Westley (Cary Elwes), two young people in love. Westley goes off to sea to earn enough money for them to marry, but Buttercup gets word that the Dread Pirate Roberts, who never leaves survivors, attacked his ship. Devastated, Buttercup agrees to wed Prince Humperdinck (Chris Sarandon), only to be kidnapped before the wedding. The fantasy elements meld beautifully with the nonstop adventure, including swashbuckling swordfights, a rhyming giant, a race through the dangerous fireswamp and a trip to a magician when they need a miracle. The love story between Buttercup and Westley is very sweet and overcomes obstacles galore for their happy ending. The movie includes a real-world frame of an old man reading the story to his sick grandson, which reminds the viewer that this is a fairy tale. Gently poking fun at the classic story-time elements and adding heaps of humor earns this romance/adventure/fantasy its cult classic status.

MORE MEDIA MIXING OF FAIRY TALE FANTASY,
ADVENTURE, AND ROMANCE

TV: *Once Upon a Time*

Book: *Good Omens* by Neil Gaiman and Terry Pratchett

Graphic novel: *Fables* by Bill Willingham

MORE FILM GENRE BLENDS

Pan's Labyrinth (historical/horror/fantasy)

Alien (SF/horror)

Big Trouble in Little China (fantasy/romance/adventure)

Inception (SF/thriller)

Dark City (mystery/SF)

From Dusk Till Dawn (thriller/horror)

Gattaca (SF/thriller/romance)

Angel Heart (horror/mystery)

Graphic Novels

Comics, including their longer-story-arc brethren graphic novels, are a unique blend of visual images and written word. The format can leverage the powerful ability of pictures to tell hugely imaginative stories while still utilizing the written word for things that images can't convey like exposition or dialogue. In many ways it is the most efficient visual storytelling medium, not limited by budgets or actors to show anything its creator can think up, but with the addition of words to help carry the narrative weight of the story. Although the stories most people associate with comics are superheroes in tights, any genre that appears in literature can be found in comics, including lots of blends of those genres. Even superhero comics, which tend to fall into the adrenaline category because of their focus on action and adventure, can be blended, such as with the overtly noir tone and crime story arc of much of the Batman family of comics. There are fantasy and SF elements to many classic superhero comics as well, but graphic novels are bigger than the iconic superhero lines. A graphic novel might blend two or more genres in order to tell new stories. Graphic storytelling is a medium with very few limits, and that includes limiting a creator to one genre.

Saga by Brian K. Vaughan (STORY) and Fiona Staples (ART)

Romeo and Juliet in space. This elevator pitch summarizes *Saga* but doesn't convey the clever world building and storytelling of this series. Two interstellar cultures have been at war for generations, but despite being on different sides of the conflict, winged Alana and horned Marko found each other and fell in love. As the series opens, Alana is hugely pregnant and the two are on the run. Soon baby Hazel is born, and the lovers will do anything to protect her. The series combines space opera and magic in much the same ways that *Star Wars* did, proving this combo has great narrative possibilities. Alana's planet of Landfall is the very technologically advanced center of galactic power while Marko's planet of Wreath is a small satellite of Landfall and his people magic wielders. Powers on both sides align against the lovers, giving the story urgency and tension. With the unfettered imagination only possible in comics, Vaughan and Staples have created a vivid world and populated it with extremely unusual characters, such as Prince Robot IV, one of those sent after Alana and Marko who happens to have a TV for a head. Visually and narratively, this is a very cool, very weird world.

MORE MEDIA MIXES

TV series that include unlikely lovers: *Beauty and the Beast*

Film interpretation of Romeo and Juliet: *Romeo + Juliet* (Luhrmann version)

Book about SF and fantasy star-crossed lovers: *Songs of Love & Death* edited by George R. R. Martin and Gardner Dozois

Watchmen by Alan Moore (STORY) and Dave Gibbon (ART)

One of the most respected collected works in comics is Alan Moore's *Watchmen*. Its structure, ostensibly, is that of a mystery with the opening issue/chapter telling readers of the recent murder of Edward Blake. Blake was once the costumed superhero The Comedian, and former teammate and fellow hero/vigilante Rorschach sets out to find out who killed him, uncovering what he believes to be a plot to kill other costumed crime fighters. From this noir setup, we explore the fate of retired superheroes called back into service. It's a dark book, both in Moore's themes of paranoia, megalomania, and impending doom and in Gibbon's gritty real-world art. The superheroes supply the other genres for *Watchmen*, most of which would fall under the category of science fiction, such as mutated super-powered Dr. Manhattan and the gadget-loving Night Owl, and, of course the overall alternate history premise of the world in which the action takes place. *Watchmen* broke ground with a lot of firsts: first mainstream comic envisioned and executed as a graphic novel with a beginning, middle, and end to the story; one of the first superhero stories written to be best appreciated by adults; first (and only) graphic novel to ever win the Hugo award for SF. It's a masterwork in any medium.

MORE MEDIA MIXES

TV with a mix of dark and gritty cityscape and costumed crime fighter: *Arrow*

Film with a mix of noir and superhero: *Batman Begins*

Book that looks at superheroes (and their families) after retirement: *After the Golden Age* by Carrie Vaughn

---

Sandman by Neil Gaiman (STORY) and various artists

This cult favorite comic series launched Neil Gaiman's career and also showcases his trademark mix of fantasy and horror. In *Preludes and Nocturnes* (the first collected volume of *Sandman*) Morpheus, the lord of Dreams, has been imprisoned by humans who were hoping to harness the power of his sibling Death. They keep him trapped for 70 years, and when he finally breaks free he must track down the three talismans of his power that have been scattered over the years. Only then will he be able to fully reclaim the dream world. A brilliant mix of dream and nightmare, with imagery (mostly drawn by Sam Keith in this volume) that is by turns lovely and grotesque. Gaiman draws extensively on mythology and fable but creates a world that is still distinctly his own. This world shares borders with the rest of the DC Comics universe, and *Preludes and Nocturnes* includes cameos from characters like John Constantine and Doctor Destiny. Gaiman explores more of the Dreamlord's world in the rest of the series, and his love of writing regular characters dealing with supernatural weirdness can be seen throughout his oeuvre. But for many, the morose lord Dream will be his quintessential creation.

MORE MEDIA MIXES

TV that mixes fantasy and horror: *Moonlight*

Film that mixes dream and nightmare: *Pan's Labyrinth*

Book that mixes myth and magic and darkness: *Dreams Underfoot* by Charles de Lint

MORE GRAPHIC NOVEL BLENDS

League of Extraordinary Gentlemen (historical/adventure)

Hellboy/B.P.R.D. (fantasy/historical/adventure/mystery)

American Vampire (historical/horror)

Chew (SF/mystery)

John Constantine, Hellblazer (fantasy/mystery)

Fables (fantasy/romance)

Powers (fantasy/mystery)

A Distant Soil (SF/fantasy/romance)

9

READERS' ADVISORY FOR BLENDS

Readers' advisory, especially in the public library, is about supporting the reading that library users do for their own enjoyment. The goal is to find the right book for the right reader. This might be done by one-on-one transactions in which a librarian works directly with the reader and the end result is the physical handoff of a stack of individually selected books to a grateful reader. Or it might be through less personal but still effective methods that include the way we display and market our collections as well as the tools and aids we provide to lead readers to books in our online catalogs and websites and even (still!) paper handouts and bookmarks. Sometimes the role of the readers' advisor is to precisely match the parameters readers have given us for the perfect book that they have been seeking. But usually there is no single perfect book. There are options and choices, some of which might exactly meet their expectations but some of which might surprise and delight them and be the book they never knew they wanted to read. Personally, when I work with readers, I try to do at least a little of both. A genre-blended book might be exactly what a reader is looking for, but it can also be the surprise book with which we tempt readers to try something new.

The first issue to tackle for readers' advisors wondering whether to suggest a blend is to know what the readers *think* they want to read. It's not our job to change their minds, force them to see the beauty of a genre they detest, or otherwise push our own agendas. But if you get readers who tell you that they read anything (great when it's true) or that they are open to multiple genres, then a blend can be something to try.

Sometimes readers actually seek out blends, especially when it comes to blends that are very popular and have so many examples that they are recognizable subgenres. For these readers, prepared booklists or access to a readers' advisory tool can be a great way to supplement subject access from the online catalog and pull together a pile of possible reads. With fans of these well-established blends, it might be most useful to remember not only that these readers might be open to other blended books, but that you can usually find blends more solidly in one genre than the other that they might enjoy. For example, with fans of historical mysteries you can find hundreds of other historical mysteries, usually even set in the same time period. These patrons might like other blends like historical thrillers or historical romances. But you can also probably find books that are contemporary mysteries or straightforward historical fiction that would appeal to these readers. It all depends on what they enjoy about those books and what reading experience they want next.

For example, let's say you are working with readers who loved Audrey Niffenegger's *The Time Traveler's Wife*. I use this as an example of a genre blend that was not marketed as such and that had a huge mainstream audience. Their enjoyment of the book might have come from the combination of a vivid science fiction premise and a romantic story line, but it might have been more one of those things than the other. Maybe they thought the time travel story of a man with a genetic condition that causes him to uncontrollably travel through time was fascinating. You could find them other SF books that either deal with time travel or another SF topic that causes personal affliction. Maybe they fell for the love story of a couple that meet and fall in love and make a life with each other despite the huge obstacle of never being sure when the man will be ripped out of time. Any big conflict romance might scratch the itch. Did the readers love the relationship but felt gutted that the protagonists didn't get a perfect happy ending? A regular romance might give them the closure they crave. Or it might be that neither genre was the appeal but instead the readers loved the characters or the writing. Reading is an incredibly personal thing, and no two people come away from a book having read it exactly the same way. So before you dive into the stacks looking for something that blended the two genres in exactly the same way, make sure you understand why someone loved a book.

As discussed in the introduction, the audience for a blend could be really large or really small depending on how well the blend works. It could be a book you could hand to everyone who loves either genre, or it could end up a book that would only appeal to the people who equally love both genres. To find out whether a genre-blended book will work with fans from one of the constituent genres, it is important to have a readers' advisory conversation with them.

Take a book like *Midnight Riot* by Ben Aaronovitch, which is a mystery/fantasy blend. The real-world setting in London's Metropolitan Police force and solid police procedural structure would seem to make this blend a good thing to put in the hands of fans of the Cynthia Harrod-Eagles series featuring Inspector Bill Slider. But the supernatural goings-on with ghosts and wizards and gods that inhabit the rivers of London would seem like it should be more up the alley of fantasy fans who like Terry Pratchett. If the book was less skillfully blended and less clever with both its use of a mystery plot structure and a secret fantasy world, I would say you would have to seek out readers who read and love both genres equally. It's not impossible to find readers who juggle Harrod-Eagles and Pratchett, but they might not announce themselves to you. However, because Aaronovitch does his job of blending so well, I would be happy to try this with either fan base, pending further exploration of what that reader is in the mood for.

Examples of the kinds of questions you could ask fans of the Bill Slider series before recommending *Midnight Riot*:

> Do you like Cynthia Harrod-Eagles because of the London setting? (good match)
>
> Do you like the fast pace and witty dialogue of the series? (good match)
>
> Do you like the introspective detective and the inclusion of a romantic subplot (not as good a match)
>
> *Important final question*: Do you want to try something different?

Examples of the kinds of questions you could ask fans of Terry Pratchett before recommending *Midnight Riot*:

> Do you like Pratchett for the regular folks interacting with magic? (good match)
>
> Do you like humor in your fantasy? (good match)
>
> Do you like the elements of sometimes slapstick parody in Pratchett? (not as good a match)
>
> What's your favorite Pratchett book? (*Guards! Guards!*—good match; *Colour of Magic*—less perfect)
>
> *Important final question*: Do you want to try something different?

But further questions that don't even touch on genre could help you decide if readers would like *Midnight Riot*. Do they like fish-out-of-water stories in which characters have to adapt to a big shift in their worldview? Do they like stories with a lot of personal growth? How do they feel about stories that are violent or even a bit gruesome? Do they like stories with a fast pace that are jammed with action?

WHEN TO SUGGEST A BLEND

Many, many people self-identify as readers of a particular genre. But the very formula that draws readers back to a genre again and again can also lead to genre fatigue. Most of us have gone through it—you are a voracious consumer of a genre, and one day you just can't face another book like the books you've been reading. Cozy mystery overload. Regency romance binge hangover. Because most genres contain a multitude of different storytelling techniques, readers can wander into a different corner of a genre they've always read—swap a cozy mystery for something grittier, for example. Reading something that maintains the structure or the story beats of a genre a reader loves but adds in another genre can totally refresh the palate.

When working with readers who normally read one genre but who communicate that they are bored or uninspired to read books they normally enjoy, a readers' advisor should consider recommending a blend. To make the blend more easily acceptable, start with a genre that they already read and enjoy. For fans of fantasy, for example, start with a book that includes that genre. Then try to feel out what other genres they might sometimes read, or even a genre they've always wanted to try. Find something that still gives them some of their comfort genre of fantasy but also includes healthy doses of another genre. If you think they are hesitant to try that other genre, maybe start with the books in the fantasy chapter, as those are all fantasy-forward in their blending. If the reader is willing to dive more fully into a different genre pool, try a book from another chapter that uses fantasy as a blend element.

Recommending blended books can be a great way to expose receptive readers to whole new worlds they have never explored. A blend can be a key that unlocks a genre the reader never thought they could enjoy. Be cautious though. Although you can surely find blends that will slip in a genre in a way that bypasses most innate resistance from those who claim to have no interest in reading that genre, readers' advisors have better luck working from a starting point within a reader's stated comfort zones. That doesn't mean you can't stretch that comfort zone, but it's best to be up front about the genre elements in a suggested read. They'll trust you more the next time. Because so much of the resistance that readers put up against certain genres comes from preconceptions about what kinds of books are written in that genre, reading a blend really can change a genre skeptic's outlook. By giving readers a blend that includes something they already read and enjoy, you ease their way and allow them to set aside those preconceptions and experience the genre on its own terms.

PROMOTING GENRE BLENDS

In addition to suggesting blends in our readers' advisory work with individual readers, how else can we promote genre blends in our libraries? These are books that don't always get found. Living between genres can mean that these books can get lost in the cracks. Here are some strategies to make sure they get found.

Buy Them

Collection development issues for blends can be just as complicated as readers' advisory issues. These books might not be reviewed where you expect or might not be reviewed at all. Because more blended books are being published all the time, it is common to find these books covered in the reviewing outlets that librarians use most, and often the reviewer will mention if there is more than one blend at play in a book. But because every reader experiences a book in a unique way (even reviewers), the genre elements that jump out at one reader might be lost on another. Readers and reviewers are also influenced by the choices the publisher has made. If everything about a book's presentation says that it is one genre, the reader will often experience it as that one genre, perhaps with some added flourishes. For selectors, a blended book might also be reviewed in one genre section instead of another and get lost in the shuffle if there are multiple selectors who all believe the "other selector" will pick up that title. Just as some publishers might be hesitant to pick up a book because they are unsure whether it will find its audience, librarians can be prey to those same fears. But whereas publishers have little control over what happens to a book after they commit to it, librarians decidedly do have control. Finally, on the collection management side, when looking at blends that haven't circulated enough to earn their keep come weeding time, consider one last cross-genre promotion of the title. Perhaps you can display a dusty science fiction/mystery with your mystery collection or include a low-circulation historical romance with historical fiction set in the same time period.

Promote Them

One of the best ways to promote any title is to hand sell it in person to a reader. Your own enthusiasm for a title can often overcome any reader's initial reluctance to try a new genre-blended title. In addition to actually putting the book in a reader's hand, librarians are experts at finding other ways to make sure a good book gets noticed. These include displays, booklists, shelf talkers, blog posts, and more. When conducting more passive forms of RA, I would encourage library staff to think outside the genre box. Make connections for your library users that they might not have thought of.

DISPLAYS

Displays are a great way to help books get the attention they deserve. Space concerns can limit a librarian's options for displaying materials, but a creative readers' advisor knows that a little thing like not having dedicated display space doesn't mean you can't display books. Even if you carve out only a few feet of counter space near your checkout locations, you can entice readers by propping up a few favorites. Grocery stores know what they are doing by having gum and candy at the checkouts. People are creatures of impulse and convenience. Displays are the ultimate convenience, narrowing our large collections into a smaller subset of titles that have the added benefit of being personally chosen by someone on staff. Any library not doing some kind of staff-picks display, no matter how small, is missing a great opportunity. Consider including blends in genre displays to open up whole new genres to your readers. Preparing a display of horror picks for Halloween? Throw in a blend from another genre. Even as small a thing as spinning an unusual blended book around so that it is cover out can be enough to grab the attention of a receptive browser. Would they have picked up China Miéville's *The City and the City* if they weren't grabbed by its dreamy cover with mirrored skylines? Maybe. But that sucker moves whenever I put it cover out.

BOOKLISTS

Annotated booklists are a terrific way to not only tell your users about books they might enjoy, but also give them enough information to intrigue and ensnare them. These booklists can be old-school bookmarks that are printed out and stuck in relevant books, they could be slightly fancier versions with QR codes for linkage to the online catalog, or they may be entirely online, either in a blog or a list maintained on your website. If annotating, try to remember to talk about all the genres in a blend and include how and why they work together. Have you pulled together a romance booklist? Broaden the scope by adding a blend. Even unannotated booklists and cover carousels in our online catalogs and websites can be ways to expose readers to books they might never have stumbled upon on their own. Tagging readalikes for George R. R. Martin in your online catalog? A historical fiction/fantasy blend might be a great title to tag as well.

PROMOTE ACROSS FORMAT

The possibilities of whole collection RA (discussed in chapter 8) cannot be forgotten. If there were a new movie in the *Alien* universe, I would promote SF/horror blends from the book, TV, and graphic novel collection as fast as I could.

Discuss Them

Blended books can be great to promote to book clubs and to use with a library's book discussion groups. The fact that they do not fit neatly into simply one genre can open up whole new avenues for discussion. Why did the author choose to work with the genres that he did? What does each genre bring to the story? Does the blend work? Although lots of blends could make for good fodder for a group, many book clubs focus on titles that are not explicitly genre, so titles from Appendix A (literary fiction blends) might be one of the first places to try. But there are some other genre blends that would spark some great conversations:

> *Lexicon* by Max Barry
>
> *The Yiddish Policemen's Union* by Michael Chabon
>
> *Jonathan Strange & Mr. Norrell* by Susanna Clarke
>
> *Gone Girl* by Gillian Flynn
>
> *I Am Legend* by Richard Matheson
>
> *The City and the City* by China Miéville
>
> *Child 44* by Tom Rob Smith

Make Sure People Can Find Them

As discussed in the introduction, one of the biggest challenges for genre blends is discoverability. Publishers make decisions about how they are going to market a book, and these decisions often trickle down to how we shelve and promote them in our libraries. While we don't have a lot of say in what kind of cover and jacket copy are chosen for a book, which are two of the primary ways that book browsers decide whether they're interested in a book, we do have tools that can help searchers. Fiction subject headings in our catalog are notoriously unsatisfactory when compared to those used for nonfiction works. Part of that is the nature of the beast: it is simply harder to put a label on fiction than fact. But there are things that we can do to make sure that even those who never come to a librarian directly for help still get our help in the catalog to find genre blends. One is to make sure that both genres are represented in the catalog record so that those utilizing those headings in the catalog can choose either (and with some catalog interfaces, users can choose both, which is ideal). For hybrids that are not already represented by a blend subject heading, such as "Historical Mystery" or "Paranormal Romance," consider adding additional subject headings, or at least tags to those titles. "Fantasy Mystery" or "Science Fiction Romance" might not be official subject headings in your library, but if you had access to those categories it would not take long to find dozens of titles that could happily be tagged with that heading, allowing them to be mutually discoverable by a patron who stumbles upon any one of them in your catalog. Modern catalog discovery layers often allow this kind of local tagging as well as the ability to link to library-created booklists, which can be another way to highlight titles for those users who browse our collections strictly through the catalog.

Literary Fiction Blends

Full disclosure, I have a problem with the idea of literary fiction as a genre. What critics, booksellers, librarians, and even readers mean when they say literary fiction can vary widely. For some, it is books that have reached a certain level of critical acclaim. For others, it can mean any book that is deemed "well written." It can refer to a certain serious tone, introspectiveness, or a thought-provoking narrative. The pacing is usually on the slow side. The characters are more important than the plot. My problem is that any of these characteristics can be found in each and every genre. But probably the only part of the many definitions of literary fiction that most people will agree on is that it is the *absence* of another genre.

So what to do with the books that contain some of the elements of another genre but are still considered literary fiction? I guess they get to be blends of a different kind. I highlight a few of the literary fiction/ genre blends because the crux of the problem with any kind of blend is finding ways to let readers know about books they weren't even aware they would love. Sometimes these titles are not considered genre because they've entered the canon as "classics": read in schools, beloved by all, their genre label tends to get dropped over time. Sometimes an author's reputation in literary circles will overwhelm any genre she dabbles in. Once the literary establishment has embraced an author, his books are often genre-label-resistant forevermore. The books in this section might not be labeled or shelved as genre fiction, but readers' advisors should try to remember them when working with genre fans.

Adrenaline

Night Film by Marisa Pessl

Ashley Cordova is found dead from an apparent suicide in New York City, inspiring a new wave of interest in her reclusive genius father, filmmaker Stanislas Cordova. Journalist Scott McGrath is certainly interested, as an ill-considered investigation of the filmmaker pretty much destroyed his career. As Scott picks up a couple teenage side-kicks and delves deeper and deeper into the cultish world of Cordova and his fans, readers will be on the edge of their seats. This is an intricately plotted, tension-filled departure for a young author whose previous coming-of-age novel was acclaimed by the literati. The writing is still very fine but the tone completely different as we explore the mystery of what happened to Ashley as well as what might still be happening at the remote estate belonging to Cordova. There are hints of the occult, children in peril, and through it all, a sympathetic everyman in Scott who simply can't let things go. The multiplicity of genres at play in this work would seem to limit its appeal, but the long wait for Pessl's second book meant that this book was embraced by a large audience. Cordova is often directly and implicitly referred to in the book as a horror filmmaker who transcended his genre, and it's not hard to see that Pessl's novel parallels this theme by using genre generously but finding an audience far beyond any one genre.

Pulse-raising thrillers and suspense titles that hide in the literary fiction section:

> *The Lola Quartet* by Emily St. John Mandel
>
> *Finn* by John Clinch
>
> *The Innocent* by Ian McEwan
>
> *The Club Dumas* by Arturo Perez-Reverte
>
> *Rebecca* by Daphne DuMaurier

Fantasy

The Magicians by Lev Grossman

The popularity of this book (and its sequels) beyond fantasy fandom can possibly be traced back to the Harry Potter phenomenon. In the *Magicians*, Grossman consciously echoes children's classics; not only the Potter books but also C. S. Lewis's Narnia books and

Tolkien. Calling back to favorite childhood stories is a great way to get adult readers to read a book with a fantasy plot. And despite the fact that this book was marketed squarely to mainstream readers, this *is* a fantasy. Quentin is your typical sulky, geeky teenager who grew up obsessed with a series of books about children who find a way to travel from our world to the magical land of Fillory. His life changes when he gets invited to enroll in a special school for the magically talented called Brakebills College. There, Quentin learns how to do real magic, but it is more work and less glamour than he imagined. After graduation, Quentin and his friends should be dealing with the usual realities of figuring out what to do with the rest of their lives, but everything changes again when they find out that Fillory is real. Although this book is obviously catnip for those who loved Narnia and Hogwarts, it is also full of very realistic portraits of sullen young adults drinking and drug taking and in general flailing about to find their path. Themes that resonate beyond fantasy include the general coming-of-age narrative and what to do when you get what you thought you wanted and it's not what you expected. The mix of very realistic characters and magical childhood fantasy trappings is probably a big reason this caught the general reading crowd's fancy, as is the fact that the author is known outside of the genre.

Magical, fantastical books from the literature shelves:

> *Vampires in the Lemon Grove* by Karen Russell
>
> *Some Kind of Fairy Tale* by Graham Joyce
>
> *Book of Lost Things* by John Connolly
>
> *The Golem and the Jinni* by Helene Wecker
>
> *The Brief History of the Dead* by Kevin Brockmeier

Historical

Wolf Hall by Hilary Mantel

Winner of the Booker Prize as well as a huge bestseller, *Wolf Hall* took the brilliant approach of showing us a period of history that has been well covered in literature, that of Henry VIII, through the eyes of a lesser-known personage of the time. While Thomas Cromwell is by no means a nobody—he was chief minister to the king of England, after all—details of his life and marriages are not taught in school. This gives readers a chance to feel like they are learning something new about a truly fascinating character in history, while also getting a new perspective on something they thought they knew. The efforts Henry took to be free of his first wife Katherine of Aragon in order to marry Anne Boleyn are facts in a book, but the scheming and politicking that had to happen to get Henry what he wanted makes for irresistible drama. By choosing Cromwell as her book's center, Mantel breathes new life into the story. Cromwell is also an easier person for any reader to empathize with than if she had told the story from the point of Henry or Anne, as he was lowborn and self-made and never completely comfortable in the life at court. But despite its huge appeal for literary fiction readers, this is no historical fiction-lite. Mantel throws the reader into the deep end, expecting a certain amount of knowledge about the people and politics of the time that probably sent a lot of readers scrambling to Wikipedia to brush up on the background. The writing is exquisite, which helps to explain why a book focused so narrowly on one period of time found an audience among many who would not normally read historical fiction. Having that "Booker Prize Winner" sticker on the front never hurts either.

Other historical fiction titles known (and read) by the literary crowd:

> *Restoration* by Rose Tremain
>
> *Atonement* by Ian McEwan
>
> *The English Patient* by Michael Ondaatje
>
> *Snow Falling on Cedars* by David Guterson
>
> *Cold Mountain* by Charles Frazier

Horror

Let the Right One In by John Ajvide Linqvist

Oskar is a 12-year-old boy living in 1980s Sweden who has been subjected to an escalating campaign of bullying from his schoolmates, leaving him helpless and full of rage. Distraction from his unhappy family life and bullying comes both from the discovery nearby of a body that had been drained of blood and also from a new neighbor, the mysterious Eli. Eli, who has moved next door with her father, appears to be a young girl Oskar's age, but nothing is what it seems. Eli is a centuries-old vampire, and the man posing as her father is a pedophile who hunts victims for Eli to supply her with blood. Even when Oskar discovers her nature he is still drawn to Eli, who protects him from his tormentors. This is a dark and unusual vampire story, full of a distinctly Scandinavian melancholy and loneliness. The character of Eli's human procurer, Haken, and Oskar's bullies are monstrous, but Eli is a sympathetic monster, although her hunting is a gory business. This is classic horror in its subject matter, but the way that Linqvist approaches the vampire resonated with audiences beyond horror fans. This is a classic example of something that gained a big push from being associated with a hit foreign movie—proof that people are much more open to horror in cinematic form; fans of the movie flocked to the book, which is even darker.

All the scares and tension of horror but with bonus critical acclaim:

> *The Accursed* by Joyce Carol Oates
>
> *Frankenstein* by Mary Shelley
>
> *Zone One* by Colson Whitehead
>
> *The Devil in Silver* by Victor LaValle
>
> *Haunted* by Chuck Palahniuk

Mystery

Case Histories by Kate Atkinson

A brief look at the holdings of dozens of libraries shows only a couple who put Kate Atkinson's first book featuring British detective Jackson Brodie in their mystery collections, keeping it instead on the fiction shelves. Looking at the book's premise and structure, it is hard to see why. It is an interesting question why this book appeals so strongly to general fiction readers while still being a satisfying mystery. The plot doesn't stray far from conventional mystery territory: Private Detective Brodie is asked by three separate clients to look into three cold cases in and around Cambridge. Brodie is a typical detective-hero in his broken marriage and hangdog outlook. But he is also immensely empathetic and stubbornly persistent in ferreting out the truth of these old cases. Full of humor and wicked winks at the conventions of mystery while all the while exploiting them, this is a good suggestion for non-mystery readers as a great examination of human nature and the search for emotional closure. The quirky characters of both Brodie and his clients are a plus for any reader. Last but not least, mystery lovers will rejoice in the pacing, the cleverness of the puzzle, and the red herrings that abound.

For more mysteries whose polished prose landed them in the literature sections:

> *The Secret History* by Donna Tartt
>
> *When We Were Orphans* by Kazuo Ishiguro
>
> *Shadow of the Wind* by Carlos Ruiz Zafon
>
> *Smilla's Sense of Snow* by Peter Hoeg
>
> *My Name Is Red* by Orhan Pamuk

Romance

Possession by A. S. Byatt

This novel has not one, but two love stories. Roland and Maud are two modern-day academics who fall in love while chasing down the proof of a forbidden romance between two Victorian authors. The search turns the two into literary detectives as they track down letters, journals, and poems that all tell of the love between 19th-century poets R. H. Ashe and Christabel LaMotte. The passion they discover in the past bleeds through into the present as the two researchers must work together and start to have feelings for one another. Byatt subtitled her work "A Romance," and while this is not a simple love story, being filled with puzzles and layers and not a little heartbreak, romance fans with patience for the slower pace of this one might still love it. There is even a happy ending for those who need one, if not for both couples. The language and wit of the prose, as well as the literary subject matter, mean that this Booker winner will not always be the first thing you think of for romance readers. But those who appreciate the journey to possess love will savor this layered masterpiece.

More romances for those who swear they don't read romance:

> *Persuasion* by Jane Austen
>
> *Gone with the Wind* by Margaret Mitchell
>
> *The Accidental Tourist* by Anne Tyler
>
> *Major Pettigrew's Last Stand* by Helen Simonson
>
> *North and South* by Elizabeth Gaskell

Science Fiction

The Time Traveler's Wife by **Audrey Niffenegger**

There is no good reason that this book about a man afflicted with a condition that causes him to move uncontrollably involuntarily through time is not considered science fiction. True, it is gorgeously written. The frame is very realistic, with a vivid Chicago setting and convincing details. It also has a beautiful love story at its heart, which made it a hit with romance readers and others not drawn to SF stories. Perhaps it is because the SF premise is handled so deftly, so lightly, as a *human* problem? As we get to know our time traveler, Henry, we also get to know his wife, Claire. Henry cannot control his traveling, which is caused by a genetic disorder and triggered by stress, but the time jumps often involve times that are emotionally resonant. We see how Claire and Henry meet and remeet through the years, and the connections and heart-breaking separations are presented in terms of how it impacts their relationship, rather than just as an SF trope. Time travel is a challenging SF trope to do well, but Niffenegger deftly handles the paradoxes of her premise without dwelling too long on them, making it a hit with fans of general fiction and romance fans who don't mind a less than happy-ever-after conclusion.

For more science fiction that doesn't usually get a spaceship label:

> *Replay* by Ken Grimwood
>
> *Oryx and Crake* by Margaret Atwood
>
> *Fahrenheit 451* by Ray Bradbury
>
> *1984* by George Orwell
>
> *Hard-Boiled Wonderland and the End of the World*
> by Haruki Murakami

APPENDIX B

Genre Blending MVPs

There are some authors that seem to effortlessly be able to move from genre to genre, trying on new narrative styles like one would try on a new hat. These writers can experiment with writing novels and stories in more than one genre while still recognizably maintaining their own unique voice.

Neil Gaiman

Most of the worlds Neil Gaiman creates are fantastical. They contain magical creatures, brave heroes, and vivid imaginative landscapes. But within that general heading of "Neil Gaiman—Fantasy Writer" there are many blendy things going on with his books. The comic book series *Sandman* (collected in 10 graphic novels and as of this writing revived for one more run in *Sandman: Overture*) is a great example of his primary blended style: fantasy with horror. In this work, as well as many of his other novels and stories, he delights in flipping between light and dark. He will show the reader something beautiful and strange but then show them something broken and twisted to balance the scales. He writes books in this fantasy/horror vein for all ages, including the popular fantasy/horror *Coraline* and fantasy/horror/mystery the *Graveyard Book*—both ostensibly written for children. His recent fantasy/horror work the *Ocean at the End of the Lane* is also either consciously or unconsciously a blend with literary fiction, dealing with issues of childhood fears and the regrets of adults. But versatile as he is, Gaiman has dabbled in other genres and genre blends as well. *Stardust* is high fantasy and romance; his brilliant story "A Study in Emerald" (collected in *Fragile Things*) is a horror/mystery tale; "Murder Mystery" is a story of the first crime in heaven (collected in *Smoke and*

Mirrors). He has also written episodes of science fiction TV series such as *Doctor Who* and *Babylon 5*. Whatever genre Gaiman is writing in, he brings a dark imagination and a fairy-tale-like quality. Just like his most famous creation of Morpheus from *Sandman*, Gaiman is just as likely to bring readers sweet dreams as nightmares, but he is always, always interesting.

Stephen King

King was known for years as the king of horror, a crown he earned with best seller after best seller in the 1980s. But even someone who has mastered one genre can be seduced by another. Many of King's more recent novels have dabbled in other genres, albeit with hints of darkness and decay never far away. His early blends include heavy doses of fantasy, such as *Eyes of the Dragon* and the saga of the Dark Tower that begins with the *Gunslinger* (which also has an interesting alternate Old West setting). King has written horror/SF blends such as *Dreamcatcher*, *The Stand*, and *Under the Dome*, and even a dark romance with *Lisey's Story*. Whatever genre he tackles, King's style is recognizable—well-drawn regular, everyday people caught in extraordinary situations. His good guys are likeable, his bad guys are terrifying, and the situations he puts them in take a truly twisted imagination. He has an economic style, conveying a scene in a few short lines, but where he really shines is with his deft handling of the narrative tension so important in horror. He can build suspense and evoke terror more effectively than just about any writer ever has—or probably ever will. Not every King book is a great work of literature, but they all do what they are meant to do extremely well, which is scare the pants off the reader.

Nora Roberts

The Queen of Romance earned her title fair and square, with a prolific output of romantic novels. What is interesting about Roberts, though, is the way she incorporates many other genres into her romances without compromising the essential love story. Her early category novels for romance publisher Silhouette were mostly straightforward love stories, and she has continued to write stories that are simple boy meets girl in real-world settings. But many of her best books are blends. From the In Death series of mystery/romances set more than 50 years in the future to the fantasy-tinged romantic series she puts out frequently, Roberts has found success with adding an exotic genre twist to many of her romances.

Naked in Death under the Robb pseudonym was highlighted in the mystery chapter, and the In Death series represents her most procedural books with strong mystery story lines in a futuristic setting that also contain an ongoing romantic story of the central couple Eve and Roarke. Fantasy/romance blends include the In the Garden trilogy, the Circle trilogy, and Three Sisters Island trilogy. She shades in horror to the fantasy and romance in series like the Sign of the Seven. Many of her hardcover new releases under the Roberts name in recent years have been romantic suspense, with tension and action to complement the love story. Whatever genre she is writing in, you can tell a Nora Roberts book from the way she draws her strong kick-ass female characters (and the sexy men who fall for them) and her flair for funny, sarcastic dialogue.

Lois McMaster Bujold

In the speculative genres, there are few who have shown greater willingness and ability to blend in the best of other genres than Lois McMaster Bujold. Her Vorkosigan series alone (16 books at the time of this publication) contains multiple genre blends. Some are SF/romance, such as *A Civil Contract*, *Shards of Honor*, and *Captain Vorpatril's Alliance*. A few are strong SF/mysteries, such as *Cetaganda*, *Komarr*, and the novella *Mountains of Mourning*. And almost all of them are SF/adventure blends with plenty of action, including those with the military-adventure stylings of *Brothers in Arms*, *Mirror Dance*, and the *Vor Game*. If, by some impossible turn of events, you don't enjoy the Vorkosigan Saga, she has written some great fantasy series that also blend in romance. *The Curse of Chalion* is high fantasy with a strong romance subplot. And the Sharing Knife series is equally about the romance between Dag and Fawn as it is about the fantasy quest plot. Her remarkable ability to create amazing characters and then put them through hell is how you will recognize a Bujold book regardless of genre. She loves underdogs.

Honorable Mention in the Blending Hall of Fame

China Miéville	Michael Crichton
Jeff VanderMeer	Jonathan Lethem
Dan Simmons	Lauren Beukes

BIBLIOGRAPHY

BOOKS AND ARTICLES ABOUT GENRE

Baker, Sharon L. and Karen L. Wallace. 2002. *The Responsive Public Library*, 2nd ed. Libraries Unlimited.

Chabon, Michael. 2008. "Trickster in a Suit of Lights: Thoughts on the Modern Short Story," in *Maps and Legends: Reading and Writing along the Borderlands* by Michael Chabon, 13–26. San Francisco: McSweeney's.

Grossman, Lev. 2012. "Literary Revolution in the Supermarket: Genre Fiction Is Disruptive Technology" *Time* (online) http://entertainment.time.com/2012/05/23/genre-fiction-is-disruptive-technology

Saricks, Joyce. 2005. *Readers' Advisory Service in the Public Library*, 3rd ed. Chicago: American Library Association.

Saricks, Joyce. 2009. *The Readers' Advisory Guide to Genre Fiction*. 2nd ed. Chicago: American Library Association.

Smith, Erin A. 2004. "Genre Reading" in *Encyclopedia of Recreation and Leisure in America*. Ed. Gary S. Cross. Vol. 1. 391–95. Detroit: Charles Scribner's Sons.

Wyatt, Neal. 2007. *The Readers' Advisory Guide to Nonfiction*. Chicago: American Library Association.

BOOKS AND ARTICLES ABOUT GENRE BLENDING

Halter, Ed. 2009. Interview: John Crowley. *Believer* 7:4 (May 2009). www.believermag.com/issues/200905/?read=interview_crowley

Land, Carla. 2005. *Wait—What IS This Book Anyway? Genre Blending in YA Lit*. www.yalsa.ala.org/thehub/2012/10/05/wait-what-is-this-book-anyway-genre-blending-in-ya-li

Sherman, Delia. *An Introduction to Interstitial Arts: Life on the Border*. www.interstitialarts.org/what/intro_toIA.html

Sherman, Delia and Christopher Barzak. 2009. *Interfictions 2: An Anthology of Interstitial Writing*. Boston, MA: Interstitial Arts Foundation; [Northampton, MA]: Distributed to the trade by Small Beer Press through Consortium.

Sherman, Delia and Theodora Goss. 2007. *Interfictions: An Anthology of Interstitial Writing*. Boston, MA: Interstitial Arts Foundation; [Northampton, MA]: Distributed to the trade by Small Beer Press through Consortium.

Wendig, Chuck. 2012. *The Death of Genre: Drifting Toward a Post-Genre Future*. http://terribleminds.com/ramble/2012/09/05/the-death-of-genre-drifting-toward-a-post-genre-future

INDEX